# My One-Eyed, Three-Legged Therapist

# NEW DIRECTIONS IN THE HUMAN-ANIMAL BOND

A dynamic relationship has always existed between people and animals. Each influences the psychological and physiological state of the other. Published in collaboration with Purdue University's College of Veterinary Medicine, New Directions in the Human-Animal Bond expands our knowledge of the interrelationships between people, animals, and their environment. Scholarly works, memoirs, practitioner guides, and books written for a general audience are welcomed on all aspects of human-animal interaction and welfare.

SERIES EDITOR

Alan M. Beck, Purdue University

OTHER TITLES IN THIS SERIES

# My One-Eyed, Three-Legged Therapist

## How My Cat Clio Saved Me

Kathy M. Finley

Purdue University Press • West Lafayette, Indiana

Cataloging-in-Publication Data is available from the Library of Congress.

978-1-61249-873-7 (paperback)

978-1-61249-874-4 (epub)

978-1-61249-875-1 (epdf)

Cover image: catinside/iStock via Getty Images

*This book is dedicated to all those who care, heal, and advocate for animals. Your work not only benefits animals but helps improve the lives of those who care for them.*

Clio

# Contents

# Prologue

*Since each of us is blessed with only one life, why not live it with a cat?*
— ROBERT STEARNS

*Authors like cats because they are such quiet, lovable, wise creatures, and cats like authors for the same reasons.*
— ROBERTSON DAVIES

ALTHOUGH THIS BOOK IS TECHNICALLY A MEMOIR, IT'S JUST AS much about a three-legged, one-eyed cat named Clio—an adorable, spunky gray-and-white feline who changed my life by bringing my mother and me closer and helping me to regain my self-esteem, the courage to face life's challenges, and the belief that none of us are truly alone.

The same scenario played out every Sunday in the kitchen as my mother, who was living with us at the time, conversed with Clio.

My mother would say, "Clio, let's see what Garfield and Mooch [in the *Mutts* comic strip] are up to." Grabbing the paper as she took a can of tuna and the can opener from the cupboard, my mother would continue the conversation with Clio. "How about some tuna? Kathy's in the shower. She'll never know."

After Clio finished gorging on tuna, my mother would quickly dispose of the evidence.

My almost-deaf mother would talk very loudly. But even had I not heard the conversation, I would have known about the clandestine tuna feedings because from the moment I entered the shower until I exited, the smell of fish permeated the house. After getting dressed, I would join my mother and Clio in the kitchen.

"Morning. What's up?" I would say.

"Oh, nothing. You need to read *Garfield* and *Mutts*—really funny this morning."

"More so than last week?"

"Oh, yeah. Way more. They remind me of Clio."

Then I would sit down, drink a cup of coffee, and read the paper. I feigned ignorance about the tuna feedings, which gave my mother joy in thinking that she and Clio had gotten away with something.

Clio was the center of not only my mother's universe, but also mine. At the time Clio entered my life, I had just left an abusive marriage. In the years following my acrimonious divorce, my life took many twists and turns. My mother had a bad accident, I acquired a second cat (Dickens), I met a wonderful man and remarried, my mother moved in with us shortly after we were married, the Great Recession adversely affected my job at the time, my mother had a stroke, and I had a health scare. During that same time, Clio faced health issues that left her a "special needs" cat. Watching her cope with these challenges and overcome her disabilities helped me to put my life in perspective.

My love of cats and respect for the profound impact that animals have on people dates back to childhood. I lost my father at an early age, which threw my mother and me into poverty and shattered my self-esteem. As a result, I was bullied in school and at one point even contemplated suicide. Fortunately, during my childhood and young adulthood, I had a cat who helped me endure these adversities and gave me a reason to live. Then I married an abusive man who isolated me from my mother and friends and refused to have any pets.

While several other pets have changed my life and taught me valuable lessons, none has had as big an impact on my life as Clio and her adoptive brother, Dickens. Both Clio and Dickens helped me through tough times and taught me that we can prevail no matter our handicap or what life throws at us.

According to the ASPCA, 3.2 million cats end up in shelters each year. Of that number, 860,000 are euthanized annually. A percentage of those cats are disabled or have special needs and are not adopted because of the care they require. We look at these animals as victims who need rescuing, and indeed we do need to rescue them. However, they are often the ones who end up giving us as much, if not more, than we give them and teaching us important lessons. Hopefully this book will help readers appreciate the strength of the human-animal bond and recognize the benefits of pet adoption for both the animal and the human. I also hope readers will see the mutual benefits of adopting a special needs animal or continuing to care for a pet when he or she develops special needs.

This book is in honor of Clio, Dickens, and all the other pets in my life—and yours. My pets have been an inspiration to me, loved me unconditionally, and been there when no one else cared. They have been friends who amazed me, helped me to grow, and enabled me to feel more connected.

Any pet parent will attest to the therapeutic value of having a pet, but now medical science as well has affirmed the health benefits of spending time with pets. Animals help improve the health of heart patients and decrease anxiety, blood pressure, and stress in humans. Cats in particular have a healing and calming effect on people with medical and mental health conditions.

Every day, we read stories of pets who have saved people or inspired them. What follows is my own story of how I opened my heart to a spirited, self-confident little cat and how she loved, healed, and saved me. I hope this book will inspire others to open their wounded hearts and souls to pets, to rescue them, and then to give them a chance to do what they do best—loving, healing, and saving us.

# Self-Proclaimed
# Queen of the Universe

*Cats invented self-esteem. There is not an insecure
bone in their bodies.* —ERMA BOMBECK

A FEW DAYS AFTER I TURNED FORTY, I FACED A HUGE AMOUNT OF
stress both professionally and personally. I had just returned from a
grueling weeklong board meeting and conference for my employer to
a mountain of work. On the personal level, I faced nasty divorce proceedings and the realization that my fifteen-year marriage was over,
as well as the added stress of knowing that my financial well-being
depended upon me keeping my job even though it required extensive
travel and long workweeks.

Anyone who has ever worked for a national nonprofit organization with a volunteer board of directors knows how difficult the job
can be. Aside from the constant pressure of raising money and dealing with a shortage of staff, nonprofit leaders often juggle competing
needs of a diverse group of individuals. Although I thoroughly enjoyed
working with this nonprofit group of independent business owners
who provided healthy and fun entertainment for children, they were
very demanding. It took weeks to prepare for the two-and-a-half-day
board meeting (which ran from 7:00 a.m. to 10:00 p.m. every day) and
the three-day conference that followed. Since the organization was

previously defrauded and in financial trouble, I had to justify every expense, including the price of generic toilet paper for the staff bathrooms and the cost of coffee filters in the break room.

"Can't you find an even cheaper toilet paper?" they would ask.

Or better yet, "Maybe you can limit staff to three sheets of toilet paper when they use the facilities."

"How about reusing the coffee filters and coffee in the break room? Certainly, you can get two, or maybe even three, pots of coffee by re-using the filters and grounds."

"What about the grass mowing? The lawn in front of the national headquarters building is not that big. Some of your staff may have some free time on their hands. Maybe they would enjoy the diversion of mowing the grass. Besides, they could enjoy the great outdoors."

In many ways this group brought a whole new definition to the term *micromanagement*. Spending the week with them at a board meeting and conference in Las Vegas wasn't exactly how I wanted to celebrate my birthday. However, they did provide comic relief, which I sorely needed given that my divorce was dragging on. This group never passed up an opportunity for a big bash, and my birthday proved to be the excuse they needed. Since one of my staff was at the party, I assumed there would be no more celebrations once I returned home. (After all, as they say, "What happens in Vegas stays in Vegas.") And given that I was about to be single again, I didn't need more reminders that I was also getting older.

Very few divorces are friendly, and most end up in bitter disputes over money and possessions. That certainly was the case with my divorce. My soon-to-be ex-husband (I'll use the pseudonym "Alex"), after confessing to me that he was having an affair and was no longer in love with me, had filed for divorce in March, but by November of that year we were no closer to a settlement. Moreover, the nastiness was escalating. When I returned from the board meeting in Las Vegas, I found that he had left over fifty messages in my voice mail. Although Alex was both verbally and physically abusive to me throughout the marriage, he wanted two-thirds of everything and wanted me to return to him the $50 gold wedding band he had bought at Sears. Even more galling was his demand that I give him my mother's engagement ring. She had given me her ring since Alex couldn't afford one when we got engaged, and she no longer needed it because she was a widow. Given that we lived in a no-fault, fifty-fifty divorce state, it didn't matter what he wanted financially. However, that didn't stop him from trying.

Alex also wanted 50 percent of what my aging mother, who was in poor health, owned (which was next to nothing), because we visited her on holidays. He assumed that my mother had secretly transferred ownership of her house to me. She had not, and when my lawyer and her lawyer affirmed this, Alex insisted that his presence at her home during the holidays was still worth 50 percent of the value of her house, the only asset she had. We also had visited his parents on the holidays, so I guess, given his interpretation of the state's divorce laws, I should have put in a claim on their assets. Every night I would get harassing calls from him pressuring me to accept his offer.

He would say, "If you don't settle on one-third of the assets, I'll make your life a living hell."

I would respond, "More so than you already have?"

Or if I didn't answer the phone, he'd leave messages like, "You are a stupid, fat, ugly bitch. Accept my offer. There's no way you'll ever find another husband who makes as much as I do. So, take what I'm offering."

I would think to myself, *Given the way you are acting, why would I ever want to get married again?*

My husband's behavior seemed eerily similar to the bullying I had endured during high school, except the school bullies were more polite.

I wasn't sure it could get any worse. In retrospect, the divorce was the best thing that ever happened to me, but at the time I was devastated and angry.

When Alex first left, I considered adopting a cat, but instead held out the misguided hope that he would come to his senses and return to me. If that happened, I would have to find the cat another home, and I certainly didn't want to go through that heartache. However, by the fall of that year, I realized our marriage could not be repaired, and Alex was not coming back. This was a blessing in disguise because it meant that I could get the cat I so sorely needed and wanted during my fifteen years of a cat-less marriage. I returned on a Sunday afternoon from my board meeting in Las Vegas and decided that during my lunch hour the next day, I would go to the local animal shelter and adopt one.

To my surprise, when I arrived at work that Monday, I found that my staff had decorated the office with all the usual over-the-hill birthday stuff. Black balloons, dried flowers, and black crepe paper adorned my work area. However, the real surprise was my very unusual birthday present: a little gray-and-white kitten who could fit in the palm of my hand. My staff told me she was the runt of the litter, and since no one else wanted to adopt her, they thought she would make a good companion for me.

As I soon would find out, this runt had spunk and was no ordinary cat.

During my childhood, I had a beautiful long-haired, gray-and-white male cat I mistakenly named Lisa who likewise had spunk and who helped me survive my father's death and endure years of bullying in school. I asked my staff if they knew that. They didn't. How strange that the cat they would choose for me would be gray and white and marked very similarly to the cat I had as a child.

My mother and I had never been deeply religious. In fact, I sometimes questioned whether there even was a God or superior being, or at least a benevolent one. However, now I wondered if perhaps this *was* divine intervention. Maybe God, or some higher being, did exist, and he was watching over me. Cats seemed to appear in my life during my most troubling times. Did God know how much I loved cats? Was it possible that cats were little angels sent by him? Who knows for sure, but one thing I did know was that never again would I spend another day in my life without a cat. A condition of any future relationship would be "Must love cats."

As I briefly reflected on my past and contemplated why a gray-and-white cat had again entered my life, I realized that I had already fallen in love with this tiny creature. I couldn't take my eyes off her and couldn't stop stroking her soft fur. As I petted her, I noticed that on her back was a gray heart—how appropriate for such a sweet kitten who I sensed would fill my life with love. Adulation aside, I now had to move on to the task at hand—caring for this adorable kitten. I would have no time to think about my pending divorce or the challenges of my job. I had a newfound friend, and I would focus my attention on her.

I had to keep the tiny ball of fur in my office until I went home that evening. During my first day with her, I could see that she had an attitude, possessed wild amounts of self-esteem, and was not in any way an ordinary cat. I briefly left her alone on my desk, and when I came back, she was walking across my computer keyboard. While I was gone, she had typed forty-two pages and made a mess of my desk—paper clips and rubber bands removed from their containers and papers scattered everywhere. In short, it looked like a tornado had ripped through my office. She looked at me as if to say, "*Whaaat?* The stuff on your desk needed reorganizing." But she was so cute, and I didn't care that this tiny kitten who weighed less than eight ounces had trashed my office. Who could be angry with her for long? She was just being herself—as silly as that was—and that was fine because what she did over the coming months was to show me that it's okay to be yourself and even to look silly at times. It was as if she was saying to me, "Look at me! I'm myself, and everyone loves me!" I didn't know it yet, but this tiny feline would help me rebuild my self-esteem, develop my self-confidence, regain my sense of humor, and fill my lonely hours with entertainment and companionship.

Before taking my new little birthday present home, I made an appointment with Dr. David Fenoglio ("Dr. Dave"), a veterinarian who had a clinic around the corner from my office. She checked out fine, and he confirmed that she was a healthy female except for a slight heart murmur, which Dr. Dave thought she might eventually outgrow. We discussed that I should bring her in to be spayed in a few months. Little did I know that over the course of this little cat's life, we would be paying many visits to Dr. Dave.

When I arrived home that evening, I faced two tasks: calling my mother to tell her about my birthday present and finding an appropriate name for my new furry friend. Since my mother and I had grown apart during my tumultuous marriage as my ex-husband alienated me from my family, this was a good first step in strengthening our relationship and restoring the close bond we once had. I felt that by now she had forgiven me for not telling her about Alex's abusive and controlling behavior. Cats had brought us close together before. I was hoping a cat would bring us together again.

When she answered the phone, I said, "Guess what my staff got me for my birthday?"

"What?" she asked.

"A little gray-and-white kitten, and she looks just like Lisa."

"Just like Lisa? Lisa was so beautiful."

"Yep, just like Lisa, except this time she really is a female."

My mother chuckled and said, "Oh, I can't wait to see her."

Then we spent almost an hour on the phone reminiscing about Lisa.

My next daunting task was to find an appropriate name for my newfound friend. Now that Dr. Dave had confirmed she was a female, I would not be making the same mistake of giving her a gender-inappropriate name. However, I felt that she needed a special name, not a name arrived at spontaneously or one that was trite, like Fluffy or Miss Kitty. It's amazing how long cat owners can ponder correct names for their cats. In fact, English poet T. S. Eliot, in his book *Old Possum's Book of Practical Cats* (1939), noted: "The Naming of Cats is a difficult matter. It isn't just one of your holiday games." Eliot added that cats have three names: the everyday name the family uses, the unique name no one outside the family uses, and "the name that no human research can discover—but THE CAT HIMSELF KNOWS, and will never confess"—or the "deep and inscrutable singular name." Finding that name became my quest over the next few days. Fortunately, there are several books written about appropriate cat names, and I confess that I bought two of them.

One of my staff had suggested I give her a regal name to match her personality. The first names that came to my mind were Cleo and Clio. The idea of naming her after the queen of the Nile made sense, but I really liked Clio because she was the Greek muse or goddess of history, and I had majored in history in college. I had also majored in marketing in graduate school, and the American Marketing Association gave out the Clio Awards for advertising.

❧

Over the years, I called Clio by several nicknames, including KiKi, Bunny, and Buggy, but she answered to neither her given name nor these nicknames. In fact, she answered to one word only, and that was *tuna*, which I soon discovered she loved to eat more than anything else. Sometimes I thought that Tuna should have been her name and that all of my efforts at finding the right name were for naught. I think I discovered what T. S. Eliot did not: Tuna must have been "the name that no human research can discover—but THE CAT HIMSELF KNOWS." Or at least it was the name Clio knew, and the one she knew would get her the food she loved.

Whether or not she accepted her given name, Clio seemed to be the most appropriate name for her since I would soon learn that she was a master self-promoter and self-proclaimed queen of the universe.

# 2

# Small, but Mighty

*The smallest feline is a masterpiece.*
—LEONARDO DA VINCI

CLIO WAS A SMALL KITTEN BECAUSE SHE HAD BEEN THE RUNT OF the litter. In fact, she was so tiny that I had to be careful not to crush her at night when she slept next to me. However, her small stature didn't prevent her from being self-confident, feisty, and athletic. Despite being little, she felt she could take on anyone no matter how big. We enjoyed play fighting, and many times I went to work with scratches all over my hands. Obviously, she won most of the fights. Clio loved cat toys whether or not they contained catnip. Her first toy was a stuffed worm bigger than she was. Clio would endlessly throw the worm up in the air, run after it, grab it, and then wrestle with it as if it were alive and putting up quite the struggle. When she caught it, she would carry it around the house like it was her trophy from a long and arduous hunting trip.

I soon found out that Clio loved playing with glitter balls. She would spend her waking hours chasing them all over the house. Unfortunately, a good number of her waking hours were in the middle of the night, when I would hear her chasing the glitter balls. So much for the myth that cats sleep eighteen hours a day. When one rolled under a dresser or sofa, she would come in the bedroom and meow until I got up to fetch it for her. I always suspected that she could have retrieved the ball herself and I was being played, but I really didn't mind (that is, until the alarm clock went off the next morning).

I bought Clio's glitter balls in a craft store. They came in packets of fifty or a hundred, and I would continuously have to replenish her supply because sometimes I could not find even one in the house. In fact, I bought so many glitter balls that one of the clerks at the craft store remarked, "Wow, you must have a booming craft business to need so many of these so often. Someday you should bring in some of these glitter ball creations."

Of course I didn't want to admit to her that they were for my cat and so replied, "Yes, my need for these is really growing."

For the longest time I couldn't figure out where Clio was hiding the hundreds of glitter balls I had purchased for her. Then one day I discovered a tear in the fabric on the underside of the love seat. The love seat was low to the ground and Clio was not able to fit under it, but somehow she would bat the balls under in such a way that they would pass through the tear and land inside. I was amazed to find hundreds of glitter balls inside the love seat, and a whole new definition for the term *overstuffed furniture*. It was at that point I wished I knew what crafters use these balls for because my inventory in my "booming craft business" certainly would have received quite a boost.

Early on, I noticed that Clio was extremely athletic. Perhaps in a former life she was an Olympic gold medalist. She liked to walk up next to the couch, tuck her head between her legs, and do a somersault. The first time she did one, I clapped loudly. She loved the attention and would frequently do another. Most people I told could not believe she did somersaults, and of course she, like most self-respecting cats, wouldn't do them on command. However, when one of my friends was visiting, I told him about Clio's unusual talent. He was a great cat lover, but I could tell by the look on his face that he thought I was making it all up.

"Kathy," he said, "have you thought about getting away for a while? I know these past months have been difficult." (My divorce had gone through in December.)

"No, really. She does somersaults . . ."

"Kathy, don't do this to yourself. You really have been under a lot of—"

Then, before my friend could finish his sentence, Clio casually walked over to the couch, looked back at us, and did one of her perfectly executed somersaults. My friend was amazed, and I was vindicated. Clio liked attention, and when no one was giving her the attention she felt she deserved, she would do something to get that attention. I always felt that perhaps in yet another of her lives she had been an actress.

As Clio's antics multiplied, my impending divorce no longer dominated my thoughts. Some of her pranks may have resulted from the fact that she was taken away from her mother too early. Her hunting skills were only partially developed, which I found out one cool fall night when a small field mouse made its way into my house. As I sat in bed reading, I could hear Clio running across the hardwood floors. I thought she was playing with one of her glitter balls, but then she ran into my room and jumped on the bed with a live mouse in her mouth. She didn't know that cats are supposed to kill their prey, not just catch it. As she jumped up on the bed, proud of her catch, she lost her grip on the mouse and released it. Of course both Clio and the mouse were startled when I jumped out of bed screaming. I am not sure which of the three of us was more scared. Clio took off after the mouse, but to no avail. I finally had to bring her into the bedroom, close the door, and put a towel under it so we would have no more Olympic mouse chasing for the night. The next day I went out to buy a mousetrap. However, since the poor little mouse was so cute, reminded me of a "pet mouse" I had as a child, and had endured Clio's harassment, I bought a humane trap that allowed me to release him outdoors. Never had I seen any animal run so fast once I opened the trap.

Not being able to kill her prey didn't stop Clio from hunting. I cannot even begin to count the number of nights she spent in relentless pursuit of a fly. In fact, some mornings I would wake up and find half the items from my kitchen counter or table on the floor because of Clio's inability to give up the chase. On those mornings when I did find a dead fly, I did not believe the death was due to Clio's hunting prowess but rather to the fly having a heart attack after being relentlessly pursued.

Trouble seemed to be Clio's middle name. In fact, I even added the initial *T* to her full name (my surname of course being her last name) to indicate that trouble was in her DNA. From the day she moved in, she would always follow me into the bathroom. She loved to play no matter where we were. When I sat on the toilet, she would paw at my leg, wanting me to play with her. On one occasion I was in a hurry, so I gently pushed Clio aside as I got up from the toilet and flushed. Just when the water and the contents started swirling around, Clio, who was still small enough to sit in the palm of my hand, jumped into the toilet bowl and joined the swirl. For one split second I thought, *I have to put my hand in the toilet bowl to retrieve her. Yuck.* But I did it even though she was drenched, with pieces of toilet paper hanging from her ears. Poor little Clio received her first bath that day, and never again did she go near the toilet bowl.

Clio loved to play with yarn. One day as I was cleaning the kitchen, in an effort to keep her away from the harmful chemicals she kept trying to lick, I gave her a ball of yarn so she could entertain herself. It worked, or at least initially. For almost an hour she chased the ball of yarn all over the house. Then she picked it up and took it to the bedroom. Eventually I noticed how quiet the house was and realized I had not seen Clio for a while. I went to the bedroom to check on her and to my amazement found her literally tied to the leg of the bed, unable to liberate herself. I had never seen anything like it and could picture her continuing to play with the yarn as she wound it around herself and the bedpost. Given her self-confidence, Clio probably thought she could get out of this mess herself, but instead she kept making it worse. It took me five minutes to free her from the bedpost.

Clio also loved boxes, and there was no box she believed was too small for her to fit into. Therefore I was not too surprised one day when I found her running blindly through the house with a snack-sized raisin box stuck on her head. The problem was that she was running so fast I had trouble catching her. Her first instinct was to hide under the bed, and no amount of coaxing from me could get her to come out. Since the bed was low to the ground and she had positioned herself under the center, reaching and freeing her was no easy feat. And once I did, I had to extricate myself, which proved even more difficult. To this day I wonder how she was able to get her head into that tiny box.

Clio's escapades didn't end there. Prior to an early morning business trip, I was packing at midnight to go out of town for my employer's annual conference and board meeting. I was taking one of the suitcases out to the car when Clio slipped between my legs and ran into the garage. This was a game called "Catch Me If You Can." It wasn't until two o'clock that I managed to extract her from under my car. Her fur was full of oil and dirt, as were my clothes and hair, and I had to give her a bath in the sink to remove both and take an unscheduled late-night shower myself. I finally got to bed at three in the morning and had to leave at six for a flight to Las Vegas and a long workweek. The good news is that Clio never again went into the garage.

For the most part, Clio did learn a lesson when one of her antics turned out badly for her, but that didn't stop her from moving on to something similar, and on occasion she would make the same mistake again. Clio loved her glitter balls and would chase them everywhere. It wasn't too long before she realized that if she batted a ball under the desk in my bedroom, I would get a yardstick and retrieve it for her. And if she immediately did it again, I would retrieve it again, and again. One day, tired of this game, I decided to teach Clio a lesson. When she batted her glitter ball under the desk, I didn't retrieve it for her, thinking maybe she would learn not to do that. But that's not how it went. Clio decided that since I wouldn't retrieve her glitter ball, she would have to take matters into her own paws, so she crawled under the desk to retrieve it herself. The problem was that Clio was now too big to be under there and could not get back out. I had to take out the drawers and lift the desk to free her. Once she was free and I left the room, she decided to go back under the desk since I hadn't retrieved her glitter ball. The only one who learned a lesson that day was me when I realized that teaching Clio a lesson would be difficult, if not impossible. Yet, I continued to try.

Another example of me learning a lesson rather than Clio occurred shortly after I had new windows installed in my house. I was so glad to finally have functional windows I could open. Clio loved sitting on the windowsill, smelling the air with her cute little pink nose twitching and pressed up against the screen. Little did I know that she had slowly worked the plastic pegs on the screen out of their holes. One day while I was in the bedroom working on the computer, Clio jumped up on the screen to try to catch a bird that flew by. Much to my surprise and horror (and probably hers), the screen fell out of the window and on to a bush, with Clio sitting on top. Luckily, she was so startled that I was able to quickly scoop her up and close the window. From then on, my new "functional" windows became semi-functional because I could leave them open only an inch or two. Now that Clio had found a way out of the house, I occasionally would see her trying to work the screen pegs out of their holes with her paw, but fortunately she couldn't fit through the two inches of open window.

After six months, I took Clio to Dr. Dave to have her spayed. Everything went well with the surgery, but when I picked her up the next day, Dr. Dave told me she was so angry about being in a cage that she had pawed at the bars until she injured herself. Her front paw was swollen to almost double its size. Dr. Dave sent me home with Clio and a bottle of antibiotics.

When we got home it was lunchtime. I put Clio on the couch in the den and returned with a tuna salad sandwich. Of course Clio was always begging food from me, and she would attempt to walk across my plate when she felt that I wasn't meeting her needs quickly enough. But this was the first time since I adopted her that I was eating tuna, so I had no idea how much she loved it. The surgery and the injured paw had not affected her appetite in the least bit, and she pestered me enough that I gave up most of the tuna in my sandwich. It was becoming clear that Clio could get away with anything, and because she was so cute and sweet, I could never be angry with her, or at least not for long. It also soon became very apparent that Clio would do anything for tuna and would eat it straight from a can or right off a sandwich, even if it meant that the tuna was covered with mayonnaise and she had to spit out the celery.

Clio's postoperative bad behavior didn't end that day with eating my tuna. After lunch, I relaxed on the couch and decided to sew a button on a blouse. Clio was curled up next to me, snoring and sleeping soundly. At around two o'clock, I got up to fix a cup of tea. When I came back, I noticed pieces of thread on the couch. At first I thought they were from my sewing, but when I looked closely, I realized they were Clio's stitches. When I picked her up, to my horror I saw that she had removed all of the stitches from her stomach in the two minutes it took me to fix a cup a tea. I panicked, and since it was well past the time of Dr. Dave's weekend office hours, I called the emergency vet clinic.

When the vet came to the phone, I pleaded, "Can you help me? My cat just pulled out all her stitches in her stomach, and her wound is gaping. Can you take us in, and will she be okay by the time I get there?"

"Well, there is a second set of stitches deeper in her stomach," the vet said. "You need to bring her in. She's not in any immediate danger, though, unless she tries to remove those, but they are hard to reach."

"I wouldn't put it past her," I told the vet. "She removed these in about two minutes."

"In that case, you'd better bring her in immediately."

I quickly wrapped her in a blanket and drove to the emergency clinic, where they stitched her up again and I had to pay a hefty vet bill (after just paying a sizable sum for having her spayed). As it turned out, this was to be the first of many medical adventures with Clio.

Yet despite her propensity for trouble, Clio provided comic relief and companionship during some difficult times. And she set a good example. Her silly antics, her uncanny ability to get into messes, and her intense love of tuna were what made her unique. If this cute runt of the litter had no problem with being herself, then why should I? The days and months passed, and as my love for Clio grew, so did my self-confidence and self-esteem. Yes, I was single again, but I had a companion who loved me and who wasn't constantly belittling me, yelling at me, and making me feel worthless and unloved. Yes, I had made mistakes in my life, but everyone does, and I didn't need to beat myself up over it.

Because of Clio, I began to rebuild the close relationships I once had with my mother and my friends. And that is exactly what my childhood cat, Lisa, had done for me. Lisa had come into my life at a low point, provided me companionship, improved my relationship with my mother, and given me new hope. I often believed Lisa may have been an angel sent to look over me during my childhood. Perhaps Clio, too, was sent to me for the same reason, and to give me a chance to learn again the lessons Lisa had taught me and to remember how difficult life could be without a cat.

# 3

# Lonely, Poor, and Bullied

*Until one has loved an animal, a part of one's soul remains
unawakened.* — ANATOLE FRANCE

WHY DID I DEVELOP SUCH A STRONG BOND WITH A SPUNKY, TUNA-
obsessed cat who had a knack for getting into trouble? Understanding
my feelings for Clio and how she improved my life requires a look
back to my childhood. The loss of my father at an early age, growing
up in poverty, and being bullied in school shattered my self-esteem
and destroyed my faith in a higher being and in humanity. But animals—both dogs and cats—helped me to feel needed and loved, and
this enabled me to come to terms with my situation in life. Except for
the fifteen years I was in an abusive marriage, pets had been a part of
my daily life and had always come to my rescue.

My first pet was a dog. My mother loved taking pictures, and one
photograph I remember was of me hugging my dog Woofie, a beagle
mix. I was so proud that my parents agreed to call him Woofie, the
name I gave him because he barked so much. Nothing gave me greater
joy than running and playing with Woofie in our backyard. Then suddenly my world turned upside down. Shortly before my eighth birthday, Woofie died, followed closely by the unexpected death of my
father. I was in second grade, and one day my neighbor, a police officer, showed up at my classroom door. He motioned for the teacher

to come out into the hall. When she came back in, she walked to my desk and asked me to come with her. My teacher said that my mother needed me at home, and I should go with my neighbor. I couldn't figure out what had happened and thought that I must have done something really bad for my police officer neighbor to come to school and personally escort me home. I was too scared to ask what I did, so I was silent during the ride home. I remember my mother was on the phone when I arrived. Covering the receiver with her hand, she asked, "Did Bob tell you what happened?" When I shook my head no, she said, "Your dad died." At age seven, I was having trouble processing what that meant. I assumed that he would eventually come back. During the funeral I understood a bit more when I saw my dad's lifeless and colorless body in the casket, but I had trouble accepting the finality of his death and why he had to leave us.

The funeral was held on a dreary September day, and afterward my mother and I went back to our home for a small gathering with family and friends. When they all left, the house seemed empty and cold. My mother and I both felt sad and alone, and I felt like no one loved me. I was angry at everyone. We weren't particularly religious, but my mother and I had both believed in God, or at least in some higher being. But the loss of both my dog and my dad within months of each other shook my belief to the core. I lashed out and said to my mother, "God doesn't exist, and if he does, he's not very nice. Why would he take my dog *and* my dad from me? God is supposed to be loving, but I see nothing *loving* in what he did to me." My mother explained that Woofie was old. He had had a long life and in fact lived longer than most beagles. But to me, she never adequately explained why my father died at the relatively young age of fifty-two. Then to make things even worse, my maternal grandfather died six months later. I continued my rants against God or whatever higher being did this to me.

I would say to my mother, "There is no God! And if there is, I hate him." My mother would say, "Don't you ever, *ever* say that again! It's not true." But no matter how many times she would reassure me that indeed there was a God and he had a plan for us, I didn't really believe her and felt that everyone—including God, if there was one—hated me. I wondered why I couldn't be like the other kids and have a normal life. Why did this have to happen to me? Why, among all the kids in my school, was I singled out to grow up so quickly?

My father's death two months before my eighth birthday and the death of my grandfather six months later not only devastated my mother and me but also soured me not only on religion but on life. Their deaths did draw me closer to my mother, but I was always frightened that she, too, would die and I would have no one. Our school building was immediately adjacent to the local fire station, and every time I heard one of the fire trucks leave the station, my hands would become cold and clammy and my heart would race. I feared that in an hour or so my police officer neighbor would show up at my classroom door, ask that the teacher step outside, and then I would be called out to the hall to be told that my mother had passed away. Fortunately, that never happened, but my father's sudden death had another adverse impact on our small family. It left us in a precarious financial situation. We had never had a lot of money, but now we had a lot less, which meant we had to significantly cut back. Our new financial circumstances meant either accepting hand-me-downs from relatives, wearing homemade clothes, or going naked. To me, the latter option seemed better than wearing my relatives' unwanted clothes, which to me looked ten years out-of-date. My mother nixed the first and last options and decided that she would sew all my clothes because, even as unfashionable as she was, she refused to let me wear hand-me-downs and announce to the world that we were poor.

Unfortunately, my mother wasn't the greatest seamstress, so these were not your ordinary homemade clothes. The sleeves she put in my dresses were always puckered, and the zippers were never quite right. I constantly heard:

"What's wrong with that zipper on your dress?"

"Why does your sleeve look so weird?"

"Doesn't your mother even know how to sew? You'd think she'd take time to learn so you wouldn't look so bad."

To make things worse, my mother bought the bargain, out-of-date fabric to match the equally out-of-date Simplicity and Butterick patterns that had been deeply discounted in the town's one and only store that sold fabric. I never owned a store-bought sweater and knew I never would because the price of sweaters was out of range for my mother's meager income from her job as a part-time cafeteria worker (and later janitor) at a local school. Since all the "cool kids" had them, I decided that I would learn to knit and make a sweater or two for myself. Unfortunately, I inherited my mother's skill in the homemaking arts. I'm not sure what I did wrong. Maybe I did a "knit one" when I should have done a "purl one," but you could tell they were homemade.

My home life, too, set me apart from others. I was first-generation American on my mother's side and second generation on my father's. My mother was Hungarian. Not only did she have an eccentric personality, but I grew up eating (and enjoying) food that no one else I knew ever heard of and being exposed to customs—like women not shaving their legs—that were indeed strange to others and sometimes even to me. My home life was vastly different than that of other kids in the small Ohio town where I grew up. Therefore it was difficult to invite kids over to our house. What ten-year-old wants to have a hearty dinner of cabbage and noodles, chicken paprikash, or kidney stew served by a woman who didn't shave her legs and constantly talked about the horrible atrocities perpetrated on her people by the Russians during suppression of the 1956 Hungarian Revolution and subsequent total takeover of the nation? I can honestly tell you, very few. Or more precisely, none.

I was a gangly kid, with arms longer than they proportionately should have been, and I was probably ten to fifteen pounds overweight. My haircut was never flattering, and my mother alternated between giving me a permanent and a pixie cut. When I started growing my hair long, it never was completely straight and had a big wave in it. Once when I tried to iron my hair, I burned it, and my mother forbade me from ever doing that again. If having poorly made, frumpy clothes, a perpetually bad hair day, and a less-than-perfect body weren't enough to set me apart from the other kids, I decided to study hard and earn all As so I could go to college, secure a good job, and not be poor anymore. Not only was I naturally nerdy, but I imposed even more nerdiness upon myself by trying to be the smartest kid in the class.

The daily abuse from my classmates often seemed intolerable. Regularly, I'd hear, "Hey, fat ass, why don't you stop eating that 'bohunk' food. Maybe you'd lose a few pounds." If they didn't pick on my weight, then it was my looks. "Even if you lose weight, we still won't like you because you're ugly and stink." During gym class, I was always the last to be chosen for any team. It didn't matter what sports team it was. Softball, basketball, volleyball, bowling . . . I was never chosen. Even when I was the only one left to be chosen and one of the teams lacked the proper number of members, I was rejected and insulted. They would say, "Do we have to take *her*? We don't want her—we hate her, and she's ugly too." I was not quite sure what looks had to do with athletic ability, but it was the reason used by my peers to keep me off their team and make me feel bad. My self-esteem, which had never been particularly high, sank to an all-time low.

By the end of sixth grade, I still had not found many friends. (Have I mentioned that I also was very shy?) There were other kids in my class who were also outcasts, and some of them turned to religion. The only person who had befriended me was one of those outcasts who was a staunch Baptist. Given my low self-esteem and the fact that I had no friends, I was looked upon as the perfect recruit. My new evangelical friend constantly asked me to attend her church. Her incessant recruitment tactics, however, had the opposite effect, pushing me even further away from religion. Yet, I continued to hang out with her because, apart from the attempts to convert me and save my sad, sinner soul, she was a nice person and one I could relate to on other levels. However, I resisted her every attempt to convert me because I had trouble believing that a benevolent God would take away a seven-year-old's father and her grandfather (not to mention her dog), or give her a body that would be the source of so much ridicule from other kids.

My sixth-grade classmates were extremely cruel that year, and I came home crying every afternoon. The last day of school was particularly bad. Not only had some kids unmercifully teased me over my clothes, my hair, my personality, my intelligence, my lack of athletic ability, and everything else that made up my very being, but during the bus ride home, I was told by my Baptist friend that I was an unrepentant sinner destined to go straight to Hell. Although my one and only friend was simply trying to guarantee an eternal life for me, she didn't make me feel particularly good about my earthly life.

As I sat down next to her, I said, "Hi. Sure glad school is out. Whatchadoin' this summer?"

"Going to Bible school," my friend replied. "Wanna come?"

"No, I don't think so."

"Are you saved?"

"What do you mean?"

"Have you accepted Jesus into your heart, and have you repented for all your sins?"

Too ashamed to tell her about my anger toward God and lack of faith, I said, "Well, I go to church . . . sometimes."

"That's not being saved. You know that you or your mother or both could die tonight, and neither one of you would go to Heaven. You'd burn in Hell."

As the bus approached my home, I rapidly jumped out of my seat.

"Call me if you want to come with me to Bible school, and remember, if you die tonight, you won't be saved!" yelled my friend.

My momentary school's-out bliss was suddenly shattered by the thought of dying that night and burning in Hell with the rest of my heathen family. Although I was angry with God because he took my father from me, I still wanted to believe that he was in Heaven and one day I would be with him again. But if my mother and I went to Hell, then I'd never see my father again.

"Bye," I said to my friend, then rapidly exited the bus with tears streaming down my face.

My mother greeted me at the door. "What's wrong?" she asked. "Why are you crying?"

"Mom, my best friend said that I'm going to die tonight and go straight to Hell."

"What? You're only twelve years old and perfectly healthy."

"Yeah, but a boy in our class died last year. He was only eleven."

"But he'd been sick all his life. Look, I love you, and I won't let anything happen to you." Hugging me, she asked, "Do you feel better now?"

"Yeah," I said halfheartedly, thinking to myself that everyone's mother loves them.

I knew that the way my luck was going, I wouldn't die that night, and instead I would be destined to be miserable. I felt like a misfit and believed that no one in this world aside from my mother loved me. Although I was conflicted about religion, this incident made me wonder whether my life would be better if indeed I became a Baptist (although it wasn't much better for my friend).

Sometimes I thought being dead would be better and maybe I should end my life, but I was too scared to commit suicide. Instead, I would ask my dad (who I hoped was in Heaven and could hear me) to arrange with God to let me die and join him. After all, I thought to myself, God had hurt me badly, and the least he could do was reunite me with my father. Maybe, just maybe, I'd wake up (well, actually not wake up) and I'd be dead. That certainly would teach those nasty kids at school, and I'd be with my father. But then, of course, I didn't want to leave my mother alone.

I wasn't sure that God existed and Heaven was real, so I continued to be miserable until a few days after summer vacation started when my life changed for the better.

# 4

# A Tomcat Named Lisa and His Companion, Oliver

*Animals are such agreeable friends—they ask no questions; they pass no criticisms.*

—GEORGE ELIOT

ON A BEAUTIFUL AND SUNNY JUNE DAY, I WALKED TO THE SIDE yard to throw food scraps on our compost pile. There I discovered two mangy young cats—one gray and white and one tabby—in the pile with all four paws voraciously eating not only chicken and pork scraps but also watermelon rinds and leftover vegetables. They were skinny and dirty, apparently homeless but not feral. They let me pet them, and once they began to purr, I picked them up and ran inside to find my mother.

"Mom! Mom! Look what I found in the compost pile. Aren't they cute? Can we keep them? They really like me. Can we keep them? *Pleeease?*" We recently had adopted a full-grown German shepherd named Shane, and although I really liked him, I was naturally drawn to cats. The mere sound of cats purring, and their soft fur, made me feel less angry, upset, and sad. For me, there was something incredibly calming about that low-pitched and finely tuned motor sound they made. So I begged again, "Mom, please let me keep them. They would make me so happy, and I promise to take care of them."

"I don't know. Shane doesn't like cats, and we'll have to figure out a way to separate them. Let me think about it."

"Mom, we don't have time to think. They're homeless. They need us. Please let me keep them."

"Well, maybe ..."

As it turned out, they weren't homeless after all. They belonged to the uncivilized neighbors next door with whom my mother had practically declared World War III. It began when they moved in with a pickup truck full of chickens. Despite their uncouth ways, my mother, being the neighborly type, went over and introduced herself. When she did, they proudly announced that they now had running water in the old farmhouse they had purchased. It wasn't actually running water, and my mother wasn't impressed.

"They called me over there to show me their running water. *Do you know what they did?*"

"No," I said. "What did they do?"

"They pulled a hose through the kitchen floorboards and proclaimed they now had running water in their house."

Every other week these neighbors did something else to infuriate my mother. For example, they painted all but one side of their house— the one that faced our home. They waited until her prized black cherries were ready for picking and stripped the tree the evening before she had planned to pick them because one of the branches was hanging over their driveway (and, therefore, they surmised that the cherries on the *entire* tree were theirs). The husband chewed tobacco, and when he walked up their long lane to their house and past our side garden, he would spit his tobacco juice on my mother's cabbage plants. Their guinea hens were constantly in our yard and would wake us at five in the morning. These people made anyone who has appeared on the reality show *Hoarders* look neat and clean. They also had a sixteen-year-old son who periodically took cats by the tail and threw them onto the roof. From my mother's viewpoint, the atrocities were never ending.

At first, when my mother thought these two cats were homeless or feral, I knew I had about a fifty-fifty chance of keeping them. However, once she found out they belonged to the neighbors she despised, I knew the cats were going to be mine.

Several weeks later, when the neighbors saw the gray-and-white cat sitting in the window, they called my mother and said, "We saw a gray-and-white cat in your bedroom window. It looks just like the cat we had. You didn't steal it, did you? It went missing a few weeks ago."

"There are a lot of gray-and-white cats in the world," my mother replied. "I got it from the humane society. And you need to stop looking in my window and mind your own business." She abruptly ended the conversation by slamming down the phone.

"Those damned neighbors are going to be the death of me yet," she said to me. She then cursed in Hungarian for a good five minutes before calming down.

I'm not sure what irritated my mother more—the fact that they didn't even remember that they'd had two cats, that they were watching our house and looking in our windows, or that they justifiably accused her of being a cat thief. Whatever upset her the most didn't matter to me. I knew that I was going to be able to keep the cats.

At a time when we were all afraid of the Soviet Union nuking us, I knew that if my mother could obtain nuclear weapons, she would use them on the neighbors. As much as she disliked the Russians for their complete takeover of Hungary in 1956, she disliked the people living next to us even more. Those two cats were the only animals—or for that matter, the only thing—I'd ever stolen. In this case, thievery felt good, especially for my mother, who felt that this was payback for her unsavory neighbors having stolen the fruit off her trees, the vegetables from her garden, and her nice, peaceful country lifestyle. In retrospect, these cats were my first rescue animals. Not only did I spare them from a miserable life, but they diverted my mother's attention from her frequent thoughts of killing the neighbors, and their love helped build my self-esteem.

As a child, I was a big fan of the television show *Green Acres*, a sitcom featuring Eddie Albert and Hungarian-born actress Eva Gabor as Oliver Wendell Douglas and Lisa Douglas, who left city life for a life in the country. There they meet with a bunch of backward country folk in Hooterville, USA. My mother could relate to the show not only because she was Hungarian, but also because she believed the country folk in *Green Acres* were sophisticated compared to the neighbors who lived next to us. My mother and I would watch the show religiously once we bought a television. Because we didn't have much money, we purchased a black-and-white TV, even though color television was popular at that time. However, because of the cost, a color TV was out of the question. Regardless, I loved the show and decided to name the long-haired, gray-and-white cat Lisa and the tabby Oliver.

It didn't take long before we realized that Lisa was a male. My mother and I discussed changing his name, but by that time Lisa had already learned his name and would come when we called him. Besides, Lisa didn't know he had a girl's name, and he ended up weighing twenty-one pounds and having wicked claws. If cats bullied each other for such things, I'm sure Lisa would have been ready and able to defend himself. I was particularly amused by country singer Johnny Cash's song "A Boy Named Sue" and briefly imagined Johnny recording "A Tomcat Named Lisa" as a sequel.

Because Lisa and Oliver were both males and never went outside, my mother didn't have them neutered. Little did we know how fierce the fights between two unneutered males could be when a female in heat showed up. And that's exactly what happened the next spring. Lisa and Oliver almost killed each other when they heard the cater-wauling outside. The fights were intense. Never in my life had I heard such horrible meowing and howling. They would chase each other through the house, and Oliver would climb the drapes to get away from Lisa. We tried to give them time to work it out, but it didn't get any better. Our furniture and house were literally being torn to shreds, and of course we could not afford new furniture and drapes. Sadly, we had to make a choice and give one of the cats away. Returning one of them to our next-door neighbors was not an option for my mother. Moreover, we would have to admit that we indeed were cat thieves.

Fortunately, my mother's friend who lived about a half mile away agreed to take one of them. I felt tabby cats never got the respect they deserved, so we initially gave away Lisa. But my mother's friend soon called and said Lisa was very unhappy and constantly wanted out, which we didn't feel would be a good idea. Lisa had no natural cam-ouflage. We reluctantly decided to give her friend Oliver and take back Lisa. Oliver ended up being an indoor/outdoor cat and for seven years paid us regular visits and made our home part of his territory. I always loved Oliver and felt so bad that we could keep only one cat. When we brought Lisa home, the first thing we did was get him neutered so he wouldn't want to go outside anymore. Oliver was probably glad that he dodged that surgery. Moreover, a new opportunity opened for him, and he could now mooch food off the neighbors.

Over the years as I was struggling to fit in at school, Lisa became my best friend, as did Oliver when he returned to our house for his regular visits. I still missed my dad, but I believed that he was now an angel in Heaven who had sent Lisa to watch over me and make sure I was happy. My anger with God and disdain for religion were slowly subsiding. Lisa also brought my mother and me closer together, as he was often a focal point for conversation. My mother was not interested in conversations about boys, rock and roll, clothes, or other items of interest to teenage girls, yet Lisa's antics provided us endless hours of discussion and laughter. I now felt truly connected and close to my mother. Moreover, this furry little creature loved me unconditionally and provided me with a sense of purpose and joy. I soon made a few more friends at school. They, too, liked Lisa, and he became part of our group get-togethers. My friends held birthday parties at our house so Lisa could be part of the fun. When I talked on the phone to my friends, they would always ask about Lisa and how he was doing. Slowly but surely, I regained my self-confidence and self-esteem. Finally, I felt loved again and no longer believed that everyone—including the God I now reluctantly believed in—was out to get me.

We had to separate Lisa from Shane, who hated cats, and from the dog who replaced him, Val (another full-grown German shepherd who didn't like cats). When the dogs weren't outside, they were in our basement. Like most cats, Lisa would tempt fate by going to the basement door and putting his nose up to the crack between the bottom of the door and the floor. When either dog would sense Lisa was there, he would come tearing up the stairs, only to be stopped by the door. Lisa would back away, but he knew he had gotten the better of the dog. Both Shane and Val would spend the next hour or so barking at the door, while Lisa lay curled up on his favorite chair in the living room.

Lisa tended to blend in with our small family and my close group of friends. For all the discord he would stir up with the dog, he wanted my mother and me to get along. If we got into an argument and started yelling at each other, Lisa would start meowing incessantly. At first the meowing would be somewhat soft and gentle, but then it would escalate as the argument became more heated. In the end, Lisa's plan worked, because inevitably one of us would say, "Let's stop fighting. It's upsetting Lisa."

My mother and I tended to forget that Lisa was a cat. One afternoon, someone called the house while Lisa was using the litter box.

"Hello," my mother said. "Well, Lisa's busy right now. He's in the litter box and can't come to the phone."

Once she hung up, I asked, "Mom, who was that for?"

"Some guy was calling for Lisa."

"Mom, Lisa's a cat. No one would call for him. The guy was probably calling for his girlfriend and dialed the wrong number."

"Oh, yeah . . ."

I felt sorry for that guy. After all, he had just found out his girlfriend was a guy and that he used a litter box instead of a toilet.

Lisa himself may have forgotten the species to which he belonged. He sometimes would recline in a chair on his back, hind legs spread wide, as if human. He also would jump into the bathroom sink to groom himself and then leave. I guess Lisa saw us bathing in the bathroom and decided, *Why should it be different for me?* He probably would have used the bathtub, but once while I was taking a bath, he decided to join me, not realizing the tub was filled with water. That was the last time he so much as sat on the rim of the bathtub.

Other animals also forgot Lisa was a cat. Lisa had a pet mouse we named Pierre. When Lisa would go out on our enclosed back porch, Pierre would sometimes show up. Lisa never chased him. Instead, he would just play with him, even letting the mouse curl up beside him. Unfortunately, the outside cats didn't have the same fondness for Pierre. One day he got out, and one of the outside cats caught and killed him. Poor Pierre. He, too, forgot that Lisa was really a cat and other cats weren't like him.

After Lisa came into my life, I was able to rebuild my self-esteem slowly but surely. There were a few setbacks, but I handled them well. One of those involved an invitation from a classmate to the senior prom. I never dated in high school, but when the senior prom rolled around, I was asked to go by a fellow classmate. Even though the guy was a bigger nerd than me, I was delighted that someone found me attractive. Because I was using the earnings from my new job to save for college, I couldn't spare any money for a prom dress. However, I didn't want to turn down the invitation. To save face, I told him that I had to work that evening (although I could have gotten off), but I would go with him to the after prom. When he picked me up, he told me he really wasn't comfortable around girls and had asked me out only because his father thought I was the smartest girl in the class and attractive, and maybe we had potential as a couple and would eventually give him grandchildren who were smart and good-looking. His comments certainly didn't help my ego, but unlike in the past, I was not devastated and just wrote them off as part of his awkwardness. The relationship went nowhere, but I felt that maybe at least one guy (albeit not my date, but the father of my date) recognized that I was smart and attractive. Moreover, I now had friends who liked me, and I had been accepted at a small liberal arts college with a full scholarship.

Initially I had difficulty making friends at college but eventually did so (and to this day still have these friends). I did well in all my courses and graduated with top honors. I even took off the few extra pounds I had gained in high school. For the first time in my life, guys started asking me out for dates and saying I was pretty. Moreover, during summer breaks, I had an enjoyable job in a small Italian restaurant and made friends with the family who owned it. I finally felt important, loved, pretty, and smart. And throughout it all, I developed a great sense of humor and the confidence to apply to graduate school and pursue a career I liked. I also began to believe that I was not alone in the universe and that a higher being was looking after me.

Throughout my personal transformation, I still came home at least once a month and during the summers was able to spend time with my mother and Lisa. My mother, Lisa, and my friends were extremely important to me. Life was good, or at least the best it had ever been. But that was about to change.

# 5

# No Cats Allowed

*I love my cats because I enjoy my home, and little by little,*
*they become its visible soul.*　　—JEAN COCTEAU

THE LOSS OF MY FATHER AT AN EARLY AGE AND THE BULLYING I
endured in school left deep scars on my psyche. As I soon discovered,
the good years I had witnessed during my last years in high school and
in college were not enough to solidify my self-esteem. Even though
I had begun to develop self-confidence, I was unaware of its fragile
nature and, subconsciously, still thought of myself as unworthy and
played the role of victim, which was the perfect combination for an
abuser in waiting.

While in graduate school, I met my first husband, Alex, who was
extremely good-looking and highly intelligent. In the back of my
mind, I viewed myself as fortunate to have attracted such a person.
Alex wooed me with candy, flowers, and stuffed animals. Although
he came from a troubled family and there were subtle signs that he
would take advantage of my fragile self-esteem, I ignored them and
fell in love. I felt sorry for Alex because his mother had spent many of
his younger years in and out of a mental hospital and he was mostly
raised by his father, who was stern and cold. I learned later that his
mother had bipolar disorder, but I was unaware of the damage this
had done to him because although my mother was eccentric, she was
not mentally ill. I had no experience with mental illness and therefore

was blindsided when it manifested itself in my husband, who in retrospect I believe had bipolar disorder too. To make matters worse, I also learned that Alex was sexually abused by his mother.

Alex and I were married a year after we met and moved out of state, away from family and friends. Because Alex appeared to be a sensitive and caring person who had suffered through a bad childhood, I opened up to him completely and told him all about my early life and what I had endured. At times he could be the sweetest and most caring person in the world, but at other times he was a cruel and violent abuser. Within a few weeks of the marriage, Alex revealed his darker side. I always felt that I could "fix" him and things would get better. They never did. The marriage was very tumultuous, and over time Alex became increasingly controlling and abusive. Once again, I was being bullied and abused, except this bully was someone who was supposed to love me.

Alex knew how much it had hurt me and how worthless I felt when classmates called me fat and ugly, and he would soon use all this insider knowledge to destroy the little self-confidence and self-esteem I had by continuously taunting me about my looks, my intelligence, and my weight. Alex quickly discerned that my self-esteem was closely tied to the fact that I did well in college, had gained the respect of my professors, and had made several friends at both college and my summer job. He also knew how much Lisa and my mother meant to me. By the end of the marriage, Alex had succeeded in alienating me from my family and friends and convincing me once again that I was fat, ugly, and stupid. He hated all my friends and would tell me repeatedly that they were morons. Added to that, he constantly told me that no one really respected me or appreciated my sense of humor.

The fights would start over something minor, but soon would escalate into shouting matches and attacks on my personal character. I'd regularly hear, "You are a moron. And you are an ugly bitch too." And, "My God, you are so fat. You look like you're pregnant. Your classmates were right about you—you are nothing but a fat, ugly piece of shit." And then to top off the verbal abuse, he'd spit on me, pull my hair, shove me into a wall, and pummel my upper arm where no one would see the bruises. He also knew that as a child I had few possessions, but I cherished the keepsakes I had from my mother, father, and grandparents. Many of our fights ended in him breaking something that had a special meaning to me. Then as he stormed out of the house I'd hear, "You ugly piece of shit. I wish I'd never married you. Hope you enjoy picking up the pieces of your grandmother's ugly jewelry box [or vase, or bowl, or whatever he could grab during his exit]."

I'd spend the next few hours sobbing and feeling ugly, stupid, fat, unloved, and ashamed of myself for attracting such a loser. A few hours later he would return, flowers in hand and begging for forgiveness. Then a few days later, when something wouldn't go his way, the scenario would repeat itself. Slowly but surely, he destroyed every ounce of my self-esteem, my relationships with family and friends, and the few material possessions I held dear. I didn't feel anyone would love me again or would believe how abusive this handsome, successful businessman really was. Moreover, how embarrassing to admit, not only to myself but to others, that I wasn't particularly good at picking a husband.

Alex would allow no living things in the house—no cats, no dogs, no plants. I would sometimes buy a houseplant just to have something living to care for. When he found it, he'd rip it out of the planter and tell me it was making a mess in the house. When I'd plant flowers outside, he would go out during one of our fights, pull the flowers up by the roots, and bring them inside to show me that he had destroyed them. He repeatedly pulled up a black tulip I had planted, but to his dismay, every year it would push through the ground and bloom. That tulip became my inspiration. Each spring over the fifteen years of our dysfunctional marriage, it came back up—stronger and more beautiful than ever. It also gave me a glimmer of hope that there was a God, or at least a higher being, looking out for me.

As for animals, Alex said he was allergic to cats, and dogs were too much trouble. In short, there was nothing allowed to live inside, or even outside, our house that would have given me any pleasure. What's worse, I had to leave Lisa with my mother after we were married (which in retrospect was a blessing since he might have ended up in a shelter). Since we lived out of state, the only time I saw Lisa was when I visited my mother. However, I couldn't really enjoy his company because if Alex went with me, my mother would have to lock Lisa in another room. I genuinely enjoyed the few times I came home alone and could spend time with Lisa. The year Lisa turned twenty-one, we went home to my mother's for Thanksgiving. My husband claimed that his allergies were even worse and wouldn't allow me to pet Lisa (although I sneaked in a petting or two). Because of his advanced age, poor Lisa had grown very skinny, and his beautiful fur had become matted. As we were leaving, I wanted to hug Lisa one last time because I knew that his time on earth was short.

My husband, however, rushed us out the door, saying, "We have to go, and you can't pet Lisa because I'll sneeze all the way back home."

"But he's old and in poor health," I replied. "I'll probably never see him again."

"I don't care. We need to go, and you are not going to pet him. I think you care more about him than me. Now get in the car, or you can walk home."

I am not insensitive to the fact that many people are allergic to cats, but I am sure that my husband's allergy was fabricated, since after we divorced he married a woman with two cats and a dog. He knew how much Lisa meant to me, and he couldn't possibly accept me caring about anyone else, or anyone else caring about me.

That dreary, rainy, and cold November day when we made the five-hour journey back to our home was the last day I would ever see Lisa. My mother called a week before Christmas, and all I could hear was crying.

"Mom, what's wrong?" I asked. "What happened?"

In between sobs, she said, "Lisa curled up on my lap while I was sitting in the recliner watching TV. I fell asleep, and when I woke up, he was dead."

I began crying too. My one true friend was gone, and I didn't get to say goodbye. However, as sad as I was at losing Lisa and not getting a chance to hug him one last time, I felt somewhat comforted knowing that he had died in the arms of one of the humans he loved. I wished I could have been there and always hoped Lisa knew that I loved him.

During our marriage, Alex also never failed to remind me that he had moved with me so I could pursue my "pathetic career" (although he had no job at the time) and that he had managed to go back to school and get an MBA and secure a high-paying job. At the same time, I, too, had obtained my MBA, while working full time. However, I decided to use my degree to further my career in the nonprofit sector. Never once did he acknowledge that I worked during this time and that the earnings from my "pathetic career," which I loved and didn't pay badly, helped him get a master's degree while he was unemployed. Once he got that high-paying job, he felt that he had me completely under his control since he had shredded every inch of my fragile self-esteem.

After years of suffering through his abuse, I did something that normally no spouse with low self-esteem and no self-confidence would ever consider doing: I secured a job that paid close to what he was earning. I was asked to head up a national nonprofit trade association that was in financial trouble. Within a year, I was able to turn the organization around, which endeared me to the board of directors. Although I hadn't fully rebuilt my self-esteem, I managed to put on a good front. That must have been too much for my husband to bear. In fact, after attending a social event for the organization, he sneered at me and said with disdain, "I can't believe how much they like you. You could kill someone, and they would still like you. They like *you*. *You* of all people. Unbelievable!"

Then after fifteen years of marriage, my husband confessed to me on Christmas Day that he had found someone else. I thought it was odd that immediately after opening presents he dashed into the den and started writing a letter.

"Who are you writing to?" I asked.

He slowly put down the pen, looked at me, and said, "There's something I need to tell you."

"What?"

"Last year when I was traveling on business, I stopped at a Bob Evans restaurant for breakfast. The hostess looked at me, and the minute I saw her, I knew that we were soul mates. She asked me out. What could I say?"

"*No, I'm married* immediately comes to mind."

"You don't understand—we're soul mates. When I met her three kids and realized that she hardly had enough money to feed them, I knew that she needed me."

"That makes no sense. She needs your money."

"It doesn't matter—I love her, and I don't love you anymore."

"So, you are throwing away fifteen years of marriage for a person who needs your money?"

I should have anticipated his response: "Well, at least she's prettier and not as fat."

I am sure Alex sensed that I was gaining enough self-confidence to realize his control over me was ending. He made one last attempt to keep me under his thumb by telling me that I could possibly save our marriage if his girlfriend could move in with us so he would have time to sort out his feelings for both of us. I rejected this offer, and he initiated divorce proceedings.

My new job should have been a time for me to celebrate and enjoy my successes, but being rejected yet again made me doubt my self-worth more than ever. Was all that he said about me true? I had few people to turn to since most of my relationships with family and friends had been seriously damaged. Once again, I was alone, felt unloved, and had very few friends. All I needed now was to have someone tell me I was an unrepentant sinner who was going to Hell when I died.

§

I again began to question my faith. *Was there really a God, or were we all alone in the universe? And if there was a God, did he even care about me?* I was back to where I was before. Yet although I seriously doubted I could love or trust anyone again, a little voice nagged at me. Maybe God had listened to my prayers. So many times after one of Alex's violent outbursts, I had asked God to take me away from him and to allow me to be in Heaven with my dad and Lisa. While God didn't take me away from him, Alex had decided to leave. My abusive husband was no longer in my life.

Fortunately, by the time my divorce was finalized, I had Clio to entertain me, keep me company, and unbeknownst to me at the time, serve as my therapist. And another cat, one who would teach me to trust again, was also about to enter my life.

# 6

# Trouble Times Two

*One is never sure, watching two cats washing each
other, whether it's affection, the taste, or a trial run
for the jugular.*　　　　　—HELEN THOMSON

BECAUSE MY JOB REQUIRED TRAVEL AND OFTEN I WOULD BE GONE
for a week or more, I had to leave Clio alone in the house with an occasional visit from a pet sitter. Although the pet sitters I hired took
good care of her, and some even stayed the night, Clio demanded
more attention. Of course many times Clio wanted attention only so
she could ignore you. Nonetheless, with each trip I took, it seemed
that Clio was getting lonelier and acting out more and more when I
returned. The pet sitters also noted how Clio would do strange things,
some of which made it hard to keep them or to attract new sitters. A
few who stayed in my house reported that she would sit on the back
of the couch in the den while they watched television. Then slowly,
inch by inch, she'd creep over and sit on top of their heads. She would
then crouch down, lean forward and tuck her head so she'd be looking them right in the eye, and then just stare at them. Most pet sitters
found this a little disconcerting.

About eighteen months after adopting Clio, I went into my office and checked my schedule for the day and realized that I had no
lunch plans. With my travel obligations steadily increasing and Clio's

behavior becoming stranger and stranger, I decided that this would be a good day to go to the local shelter and pick out a companion for her. Shortly after I checked my schedule, one of my employees arrived. I walked over to her office to say hello and to give her a message I had taken for her the previous evening after she left.

"Hi. Someone called for you last night and—"

Before I could ask why a pet carrier was in the corner of her office, she replied, "Don't get mad at me. This kitten has been hanging around my house for weeks. I can't find the owner, and I can't take in any more cats [she had five]. I'm using my lunch hour to take him to the humane society."

I wondered whether she could read my mind since she had been the driving force behind my staff's decision to give me Clio for my birthday. I certainly hadn't told her that I planned to go to the shelter that day.

Nonchalantly I said, "Let me see him." The moment she opened the carrier, I knew this cat was not going to the humane society. A cute little black kitten, probably eight to ten weeks old, ran straight to my feet. He grabbed my leg, sat down on my shoe, and began purring loudly. It was love at first sight for both of us. My next question was, "May I borrow the carrier for the evening so I can take him home?"

I knew that before I could take this kitten home, I would have to have him checked out by the vet to make sure he had no contagious diseases. It was Wednesday, however, and Dr. Dave's office was closed for the afternoon. Fortunately I found an available veterinarian devoted exclusively to the care of cats, Dr. Alice, who agreed to examine him.

I couldn't believe how madly in love I had fallen with this kitten in just a few short hours. All the way to the vet, I worried that he might have some horrible disease and I wouldn't be able to adopt him. As I sat in Dr. Alice's office, I had trouble hearing the receptionist's questions because this sweet little kitten was purring so loudly. Before long, we were in an exam room. He seemed healthy, but Dr. Alice was having trouble listening to his heart because of all the purring. In fact, he hadn't stopped since we'd left my office. Even when the doctor shoved a needle longer than he was in his leg, he continued purring.

"This is one happy cat," she said. "He's happy you are adopting him."

He may have been happy that I was adopting him, and I may have thought that Clio would be delighted to have a companion, but never was I more wrong. Clio had no idea what awaited her when I walked in the door that night with a pet carrier. Her first instinct was to run because she thought I was taking her to the vet, but then she realized that something was in there. When I opened the carrier and out walked a purring, trusting little kitten, she jumped back and immediately began hissing. At that moment it became clear to me that there were going to be challenges in establishing my new blended family. I would have to confine my new little friend to the spare bedroom, and Clio would be resigned to standing outside the bedroom hissing for hours while this sweet kitten meowed or purred, awaiting me to come in and spend some time with him.

With the two cats separated, I once again faced the task of naming my new arrival. The little guy had the spirit of a romantic poet or writer. He was a natural lover. Then I remembered that I had read somewhere that Charles Dickens, one of my favorite authors, loved cats. In doing a little research, I found out that Dickens had several cats. In fact, one of them was a black cat who supposedly would jump up on his desk and interrupt his writing. Being a cat lover, Charles Dickens didn't care. Therefore, I decided that Dickens would be the perfect name for my new cat. To Dickens the cat, a name didn't really matter. He didn't seem to care what I called him, as long as I was there to call him and to care about him.

Because Clio wasn't going to easily accept her new brother, I had to keep them separated for four weeks. When I would enter the bedroom, Dickens was ecstatic. He walked alongside me, weaving between my legs. In fact, sometimes it was difficult to not trip and fall. When I sat down, he was on my lap. When I stood up, he was by my feet. He wanted me to rub his back, and he'd grab my leg and hug it. If I had pantyhose on, he'd gently nip at my leg and tug at my hose. If I brought in work to do, he would jump in my lap as if to say, "Don't do any work. Pay attention to me." He loved it when I played with him, and he would meow loudly when I left the room.

To Clio, however, "Home Wrecker" would have been a better name for Dickens. Clio gave new meaning to the common misquote "Jealousy, thy name is woman." (Shakespeare's Hamlet actually said, "Frailty, thy name is woman," which of course did not apply to Clio.) Or perhaps the better (mis)quote would be "Jealousy, thy name is feline." Every other day or so, I'd take Dickens out of the bedroom and try to introduce him to Clio, but Clio wanted none of this nonsense. It was as if she were saying, "What do I have to do to convince you that I *do not* want another cat in this house?" However, slowly but surely, the hissing decreased and the attempts at outright murder stopped, until finally Clio realized she now had someone to dominate so she truly could be queen of the house (and possibly the universe). She also had someone she could get into trouble.

Just when I felt that I could trust the two of them together, things went terribly awry. Clio was lying at the head of the bed and Dickens at the foot, when Clio decided to walk over to Dickens and lick his neck. Dickens loved it. I'm sure he felt that finally she had accepted him, and better yet, that she loved him. As he was basking in the glow of this love, she went for his throat and I had to tear the two of them apart.

Nevertheless, within a few weeks, all was well. Clio finally accepted Dickens, and Dickens slowly accepted her position as queen. That didn't mean there weren't many fights along the way as Clio made sure Dickens knew the rules. For example, Dickens grew accustomed to joining me in bed at night. He would climb onto my chest and for several minutes lick my face with his very rough tongue. When Clio was in the room she would have none of this, and I was glad she stopped Dickens from licking my face because sometimes it went on for so long that my skin would turn bright red. But there were other ways in which Dickens showed affection toward me, like sitting on my lap and following me around, and I was sorry to see those habits end.

To Clio, my body was part of her territory, and she had to make sure she established control of this territory. Every time Dickens would get off my lap or chest, there would be a huge fight. Eventually, Dickens learned that Clio would not endure a takeover or invasion of her territory. Basically, the only part of my body Clio had not claimed was my feet, and she allowed Dickens to sleep on them at night. She also allowed me to pet Dickens and rub his back. But I was only allowed to pet Dickens in the bedroom where he had been sequestered for over six weeks. Occasionally when Clio was sound asleep in the back part of the house, Dickens would jump on my lap and risk her wrath. But the moment he heard her get up, he would jump down to avoid getting caught.

Dickens did have the good sense to stay away from Clio's tuna. Whenever I opened a can of tuna, Clio would come running from the farthest part of the house. Dickens knew that Clio took no prisoners when it came to tuna, so if he was close by, he would literally run the other way or go to his dry food bowl immediately and eat away, showing no interest in the tuna.

For Clio, it was probably fortunate that she developed her dominance early on because Dickens slowly grew into quite a hulk. Within a year he weighed sixteen pounds, and in three years he was eighteen and a half pounds. Dickens wasn't fat (or at least not in the beginning) but instead was very muscular. It was then we discovered that he was a Bombay, a feline characterized by its black shiny coat, yellow eyes, and muscular build, bred to look like a black panther. If Dickens only knew how big and powerful he was, the pecking order may have been dramatically altered. But it also may have remained the same. Dickens really wasn't into status or dominance. He was all about loving me and being loved by me. I have always said that Clio taught me that a can-do attitude is more important than size and gender, but Dickens showed me that love and enjoying the simple things in life are all that really matter. From both I learned it was perfectly fine to be myself.

Although Clio was very affectionate, she could also be manipulative. It was often her tactic for getting more food (particularly tuna) or her own way. Dickens was sweet and loving because that's the way he was. He wanted so little in life. Dickens was happy that he had a place to live and food to eat, and he didn't care if the place was fancy or the food exotic. In fact, Dickens liked plain dry food to eat and water to drink. His big treat was pet grass. As for toys, Dickens played with whatever I gave him, but most of all he loved having a piece of string and could play with that for hours.

In many ways, Dickens was like a faithful dog. When I came home from work or from running errands, I could always count on him to be waiting for me at the door. Sometimes he would sit on the dark brown rug where I kept my shoes, and I would carelessly place my briefcase on top of him. As soon as I noticed he was there (he tended to blend into the rug), I would pet him and quickly apologize. But Dickens didn't care that I occasionally placed my briefcase on him. He knew that I didn't mean it and was just glad that I had returned home. In the mornings, I would feed him before getting ready for work. He would eat and then come into the bathroom and wait patiently until I came out of the shower. He would follow me around until I sat down to eat a quick breakfast, then sit on the chair next to me, quietly purring as I ate my cereal and read the paper. When I left, I could count on him to be sitting by the door. It was as if he was saying goodbye and asking me to hurry home.

Dickens also never gave up on loving Clio. At night when they would join me in bed, Clio would occasionally go over to him and start licking his face. Dickens would look back at me as if to say, "I think she finally loves me, and it's going to be different this time." Invariably, Clio would slap Dickens and bite him on the neck. Yet Dickens remained the eternal optimist, and Clio in her own way came to care about him, especially when I wasn't there. When I would return home early from work, surprising them, I often found them sleeping together on my bed, watching birds side by side in the den window, or playing with each other.

Overall, Dickens was very trusting, and it was his trusting nature that often got him into trouble with Clio. One day when I was getting ready for work, I came out of the bathroom sooner than usual and discovered Dickens buried in the flowers in a large vase in my living room. Sure enough, Clio had the stem of a flower in her mouth and was running around the vase with it, spinning the foam flower base Dickens was perched on. It was clear that Dickens was enjoying the merry-go-round. When Clio saw me, she took off. I had foiled her plot with my timing. I'm sure she had planned to abandon ship just as I came into the living room, then Dickens would be caught and receive a scolding for destroying the silk flower arrangement. But the whole thing was so funny that I merely removed a purring Dickens from the vase and laughed all the way to work.

❧

Yes, Clio was indeed devious at times, and Dickens was gullible. And with the two of them together, my life would never be the same. I no longer had to worry about finding entertainment in my off hours or to long for companionship. These two would provide me with endless hours of entertainment and years of companionship, and along with this would come a completely new outlook on life. Laughter, which had all but disappeared from my life, returned. Being myself was okay, just as Clio was being Clio and Dickens was being Dickens. Moreover, there was nothing wrong with being loving and sometimes even a little bit gullible. Maybe too I could learn to trust and love again.

# 7

# Clio's Advice on Dating

*Beware of people who dislike cats.*
—IRISH PROVERB

TWO YEARS AFTER MY DIVORCE, A FEW OF MY FRIENDS INSISTED that I start dating. They would say:

"There are all kinds of dating sites."

"There's a singles group at the local church."

"There are dating services."

"My friend knows someone at work you might be interested in."

"Join a hiking club [I didn't like hiking], and maybe you'll meet someone."

"My cousin knows someone who just came to this country. He doesn't speak English, but he's a Pisces. That's a perfect match for a Scorpio. Of course, he may need a green card, but he is really good-looking."

To all of which I would respond, "I'm fine. I have my cats, and I'm not sure I'm ready to date."

The truth was, I wasn't sure if I could trust and love again. I seemed to attract losers, and I feared that if I wasn't careful I might find someone even worse than my ex-husband. Nevertheless, I finally decided to listen to my friends and seek human companionship. After all, despite the complicated relationship between Clio and Dickens, they did enjoy each other's company.

I had slowly regained my self-confidence, and even in the short time spent with Clio, my self-esteem had grown. No longer did I believe that I was stupid, fat, ugly, and unlovable. However, I decided that if any relationship were to flourish, the guy would have to like cats. This was a hard-and-fast rule—no exceptions.

In starting to date again, I learned that I didn't want to appear desperate or needy, or to suggest that the relationship should be taken to the next level. That was a sure way to end a relationship. I also didn't want to get into another abusive marriage and was grateful that Clio had helped me increase my self-esteem, which decreased the likelihood of that happening. I think Clio may have secretly known my rules of dating, because she took it upon herself to test all of my dates. And while looking out for the best caretaker for herself, she found the best mate for me.

On one occasion I was getting ready to go on a second date with a guy someone at work had set me up with. He was a nice guy but neutral about cats. He certainly didn't worship them, and that was Clio's number one requirement. As I exited the shower, I leaned down to pick up my dirty clothes and put them in the hamper. Strangely, I couldn't find my panties. *Well, maybe I already put them in the hamper,* I thought, although it would have been odd for me to do that without putting away the rest of my clothes. After I finished dressing, I walked out into the living room. Out of the corner of my eye, I noticed something white hanging on a basket by the fireplace. At that very moment my date rang the doorbell. Before answering the door, I walked over to the fireplace. Hanging on the basket were my panties, and there was only one way they had gotten there. Clio knew that after our date we would come back to the house and sit by the fireplace. I assume that in her mind, he was sure to see my panties hanging there and would probably run out of the house scared, thinking either I was too aggressive and/or desperate or I was a lousy housekeeper. Either way, Clio would be rid of him, and that suited her just fine. Her plan that night was foiled. We dated a few more times, but Clio ramped up her efforts to end the relationship.

On our fourth date, we sat on the floor in my house near the fireplace. My date had taken his wallet out of his pants pocket and placed it on the floor. Clio decided that she would explore his wallet, and before we knew it, she was running full speed down the hall with a twenty-dollar bill. My date thought it was rather amusing and jokingly said he wasn't totally convinced I hadn't put her up to this. Clio probably felt that this would most definitely end the relationship, but again it didn't.

Finally, on the next date, she was successful, or at least she probably thought so. As my date and I sat on the floor talking, Clio walked up behind him. His shorts must have been showing because she grabbed the elastic waist band of his BVDs, pulled it back, and *snap*.

"You stupid cat!" he yelled. "Get out of here."

I responded with, "She just wanted attention, and she's *not* stupid."

Clio knew I would have nothing to do with a guy who yelled at her (and especially someone who called this scary-smart cat *stupid*) and who didn't have enough of a sense of humor to appreciate a cat wedgie. The relationship didn't work out for reasons other than Clio's pranks, but even if had continued, I'm sure Clio had more tactics in store to put an end to it.

Like a typical feline stalking prey, Clio would wait until she found someone who not only worshiped her but catered to her every whim and found humor in her antics. She knew that I was a sucker for a man who was a cat lover, and a sucker was who she wanted.

For the most part, the men I dated after my divorce were losers, and I didn't need Clio to help me see that. Yet she made sure I knew that she didn't like most of my dates. For example, when one guy walked in the back door with me, he turned to kiss me and then promptly put his hand on my breast and said, "I'm a tit guy." Clio must have not only heard what he said but understood how sexist he was. Just as I started to push him away from me, Clio raced through the house to my rescue and ran straight into his leg, almost knocking him over. He was taken aback, removed his hand from my breast, and cursed at Clio. I asked him to leave. Obviously, neither of us were heartbroken when he never called me for another date.

Another guy I dated was very controlling, the signs of which I now recognized. After our first date he must have called me twenty to thirty times in a single evening. I didn't answer the phone, mostly because I didn't want to talk to him. A few times he left me a message like, "So, where are you? Out with another guy?" I'm not sure why I went on a second date with him, but I did. But that's all it took. When I arrived at the restaurant to meet him, he took one look at the jacket I was wearing and asked, "Is that cat hair?" "Yes, it is," I replied. "I have two cats," to which he retorted, "Oh, I can't stand cats and really you need to do a better job cleaning the cat hair off your jacket. You should get rid of those cats." *No*, I thought to myself, *I need to get rid of you.*

Not having any success meeting decent guys on my own, I decided to join a dating service since they prescreened applicants. Granted, I didn't meet any real jerks through the dating service, but after twelve dates, I also hadn't found anyone I wanted to pursue a long-term relationship with. After my contract ended, I concluded that being single with two cats was not so bad after all. Then one day the phone rang and it was a representative from the dating service. She informed me that they had found someone who shared many of the same interests as me and thought I might like to meet him. I assumed that they just wanted me to renew my contract, but she said they didn't and hoped I would consent to a date with this man named Jeff. I reluctantly said yes but assumed it would be one more guy with whom I didn't have a lot in common.

I went on several dates with Jeff and was pleasantly surprised that the dating service had not lied to me and indeed we did have a lot in common. First and foremost, he loved animals. He had never had a cat since his mother was afraid of them, but he had a dog, and his sister also loved animals. Second, we had somewhat similar childhoods. Both of us came from factory towns and were the children of blue-collar parents. We held the same political affiliation and religious beliefs. Moreover, he was the only guy I ever dated who ate (and liked) a fried bologna sandwich. Of course we had long since given those up for health reasons, but someone who had heard about fried bologna was a man after my own heart. I remember blurting out, "Oh my gosh, you like fried bologna! I never thought I'd meet anyone who did," then immediately hoping he didn't think my only criteria for a mate was a taste for highly processed, unhealthy meat products. But he didn't, and we continued to see each other.

After a few dates I determined that Jeff was neither a serial killer nor an abuser. He seemed very genuine, so I decided that he could pick me up at my house for a date instead of us meeting at a restaurant. The fact that he had never owned or been around cats worried me a little. I really liked him, but if he didn't care for cats, it would be a deal breaker. This time, there would be no exceptions despite my fond feelings for him.

When Jeff arrived, I wasn't quite ready. At that time my mother was staying with me while she recuperated from knee- and hip-replacement surgery. In many ways, my decision to have him pick me up at the house was to find out whether he liked not only me but the package deal that included my mother and two cats.

I answered the door and told him I needed to finish getting ready and would be right back. Before I left, I introduced him to my mother, who was in the den watching television, but not to the cats since they both were in hiding. I could hear Jeff's conversation with my mother. This was the first time they'd met, and within five minutes she was showing him the scar on her knee from her recent surgery and giving him her life history. When my mother liked someone, she could talk for hours; when she didn't, it was a very short conversation. To save him from a lengthy discussion of the Russian invasion of Hungary (which she never got over) and from possibly being shown her scar from her appendicitis surgery of forty years ago, I briefly came out of the bedroom and told him that I would be only a few more minutes and he could wait in the living room and play with my cats, who had now come out of hiding.

When I came back out, I found Jeff standing by an overturned love seat.

"She wanted her toy under there and—" he began.

I finished with, "—you fell for her love seat scam."

And he had. Clio had introduced herself to Jeff by batting her toy under the love seat, which was so low to the ground that a hand could barely fit under it.

The first time Clio put her toy under there, I turned the love seat on end with one hand and then tried to grab the toy. The problem was that tear in the bottom lining—the one that allowed the passage of her glitter balls. Clio dashed through it, climbing up inside where no one could reach her. Since she would be trapped if the love seat was put back down, it was a waiting game.

After this little test, I knew that Clio had picked a perfect mate for me and a perfect caretaker for herself. This was the devotion she was looking for. Jeff and I continued to date for another year, with many visits to my home. As we got to know each other over time, we found that we had even more in common than we had originally thought. He liked my mother and all my friends. Likewise, I liked his family and all his friends. Most importantly, Clio continued to endear herself to him with her many antics and loving behavior. Jeff started out in life a dog person, but a cute (and sometimes devious) little gray-and-white cat had turned him into a cat person and someone I could trust and love. Jeff and I got engaged a year after we met and were married the year after that.

# 8

# Tuna in the Morning, Tuna in the Evening, Tuna at Suppertime

*A cat isn't fussy—just so long as you remember he likes his milk in the shallow, rose-patterned saucer and his fish on the blue plate. From which he will take it, and eat it off the floor.* —ARTHUR BRIDGES

ONE OF THE RESULTS OF MY FIRST MARRIAGE WAS ALIENATION from my family. My mother, who was getting older, had considered moving in with me while I was married to Alex. She was ready to sell her home when Alex decided he didn't want her living with us. He thought it would be better if she lived in one of his rentals. My mother decided not to make the move and instead grew wary of ever moving closer to us. This was unfortunate because she had difficulty getting around and desperately needed assistance. Moreover, she felt that I had not been completely honest with her about Alex and how controlling and abusive he was, which eroded her trust in me and strained our relationship.

While growing up, I had always shared everything with my mother. When I first told her that Alex was leaving me, she asked, "Can't you work this out?" Then when I opened up about the years of abuse and admitted to her that he had a girlfriend, her response was, "Whaat??? Why didn't you tell me this before? I would have told you to leave him. I can't believe you didn't tell me this earlier. We always shared everything."

❧

Reflecting on my childhood, I remember there were three things (aside from adversity) that always brought my mother and me closer together when our relationship started to deteriorate: food, holidays, and cats. After my divorce from Alex, my mother would visit me. Then after Jeff and I married, she eventually moved in with us. It was during those visits and her stay with us that cooking, eating, and celebrating the holidays—all with cats—truly helped bring us closer together and restore those traditions most important to me.

Let's start with food, and cats. You couldn't find two cats with more opposite eating habits and tastes than Clio and Dickens. Whereas Dickens ate to live, Clio lived to eat. Eating was Clio's obsession. Perhaps this was because, as the runt of the litter, she didn't get an ample portion of her mother's milk and felt she needed to make up for it. Initially I thought maybe her excessive hunger was the result of worms, but she checked out fine. Perhaps she just liked food and was a feline connoisseur. Or better yet, she didn't want her adoptive brother to get the lion's share of the food. Because Clio was so obsessive about food, it was the latter hypothesis that I came back to again and again.

Clio didn't care for dry food, but when she ate it, she ate it so fast that she usually vomited. The only reason she would eat dry food was to make sure Dickens didn't get too much. Clio would eat almost anything if Dickens was around, and that included nonfood items such as string, yarn, pieces of paper, dust bunnies, and other things that weren't particularly good for her. She also would beg incessantly at the dinner table, and when that didn't produce results, she would jump up and take what she wanted from one of our plates. In short, her table manners were atrocious, and often the topic of conversation between my mother and me.

I'm not saying that Dickens didn't have some strange tastes in food. In fact, he had some very unusual tastes. For example, one night I was preparing dinner and using a recipe that called for V-8 juice. When I momentarily turned away, Dickens jumped up on the counter, planted his face in the bowl of V-8 juice, and began lapping it up. After that, every time I used that recipe, I would give Dickens some V-8.

Dickens's other strange taste was for curry powder. I discovered this as I was putting my spices away in our new built-in spice rack after we renovated our kitchen. Evidently the curry powder lid was not on tight, and some had spilled in the box where I had placed my spices during the renovation. I tossed the empty box on the floor, and before I knew it, Dickens was in there licking up the spilled powder. I could never quite figure out why he liked curry powder, but my husband and I joked that it may have been because Dickens was a Bombay, a breed that has its origins in India.

Dickens also was a water cat. He loved water, but he didn't drink from a bowl. Instead, he drank from a glass. Dickens had a ritual when drinking water in the kitchen. He would reach out his paw to the far side of the glass to make sure water was there, and then take a drink from the side closest to him. Dickens also loved to jump into the bathtub and meow, pleading with me to come in and turn on the water, just to a drip, so he could sit there catching the drips with his paw, or just letting the water drip onto his head and roll into his mouth.

These strange tastes of Dickens, however, paled in comparison to those of Clio, which kept my mother and me entertained for hours. I would feed Clio and Dickens twice a day. Dickens liked his dry food and water. He was satisfied with the food he received and barely begged for more. Occasionally, he ate cat grass. Modest portions and simplicity, however, were not what Clio was about. The moment I woke up at five in the morning (and sometimes earlier if she felt that five o'clock was too late for me to still be in bed), I had to either feed Clio or listen to her incessant and increasingly loud meowing. The way she meowed sounded like she was saying, in a very loud and shrill voice, "*Now!*" Of course, that meant "Feed me now." If the meowing didn't work, she would walk across the dresser and the computer table, "liberating" any loose items by pushing them onto the floor. The louder the sound when the items hit the floor, the better. As she approached fragile items and extended a paw to give them a gentle nudge, she would look at me as if to say, "Go ahead. Dare me. I'll shove them to the floor, too, if you don't get your butt out of bed." Once things escalated to this point, I would drag myself out of bed and into the kitchen to open a can of food. I'd barely have time to set the bowls down before Clio would push me out of the way, inhale her food, and then promptly move on to Dickens's bowl after she pushed him aside. It was fortunate that Dickens had simple tastes and liked dry food. Occasionally I would try to feed them their wet food in separate rooms, but it was hard to reach Dickens's bowl before Clio got there.

When my mother moved in with us, Clio continued to go to great lengths to wake me up every morning. She never bothered my mother when I was home, but when Jeff and I went on vacation, my mother would call me and say, "Do you know that Clio woke me up at three o'clock this morning to feed her? She walked all over me and then sat on my head. You really should teach her better manners."

"Mom, I tried to teach her better manners, but she's a cat."

"Well, it doesn't matter. I still love her."

During the first year after my divorce, I rarely ate a well-balanced meal and had no desire to cook. Eventually I decided that I really should start cooking again. However, cooking (and eating) proved difficult with Clio. One of the first meals I prepared was chicken paprikash with homemade dumplings, a Hungarian dish that was one of my mother's specialties and a favorite of mine. Happy that I had not lost my cooking skills (in fact, the dish turned out perfectly), I couldn't wait to eat.

I went into the den, set up a TV tray, and decided on a movie to watch while I ate dinner. Clio had been fed, but of course that didn't stop her from wanting more food. Chicken (tied with turkey) was second only to tuna—it was one of her favorite dishes. Although it was difficult for me to eat with Clio climbing all over me, I did manage to keep her off the TV tray and my plate by giving her several pieces of chicken. Eventually she settled down, seemingly satisfied, and went to sleep. Or so I thought.

Believing it was now safe to leave my plate unattended, I went to the kitchen to get another piece of bread. What a bad decision. By the time I returned, Clio was standing with all four feet in my plate, licking up the sauce and eating the onions. Her paws were now orange from the paprika, but she didn't care. In looking back at this incident, I don't think Clio was asleep. I think she waited patiently for me to leave the room so she could eat the chicken she felt she deserved. From that day on, I knew that I could not abandon my dinner plate, and if I did, it was fair game for Clio. When I told my mother about this, she laughed and was delighted that someone else besides the two of us enjoyed Hungarian food.

The great chicken paprikash incident was not the only time that Clio would devour food when I wasn't around to supervise. One Halloween, we left a dish full of candy corn on the end table. Jeff and I went out for a late dinner, and when we returned, Clio was bouncing off the walls and running full speed through the house. At first we thought she may have been lonely in our absence and just wanted us to play with her. Then we noticed that the candy dish had only one half-eaten piece of candy corn in it. Neither my husband nor I had eaten any of it, and my mother had gone to bed before we left and was sound asleep when we returned. Clio had obviously eaten enough to keep a person awake for hours. She didn't come down from her sugar high until two in the morning, and we never again left out any type of food because we knew she would eat anything.

Despite her bad table manners, it was difficult to resist Clio's charms. Many times when I would be eating at the dinner table, she would be sitting on the floor, looking up at me and cocking her head as she slowly licked her chops. I kept telling myself that it wasn't good to feed her table scraps, but when it came to chicken, turkey, and tuna, it was hard not to give her a piece or two (or twenty). Clio just didn't know when to stop eating. When I didn't give in to her cuteness, she would jump up on the table, and I would have to push her away from my plate. Or she would lie down on the table and then, when I momentarily looked away, reach for the plate until she managed to snag a morsel of my food with her paw. (Dickens was exactly the opposite. Only on a few occasions did he ever beg for food from the table, and I think in those instances Clio had told him it was un-catlike not to.)

Preparing Thanksgiving or Christmas dinner was always a challenge. For both holidays, Clio knew that turkey was on the menu. She would plant herself by the refrigerator until I took the big bird out to prepare it. I'm sure Clio believed that we were preparing the turkey for her, even though the bird was twice her size. After I put the turkey in the oven, Clio would hang out there, just savoring the smells. I would check on the turkey, and she was right there, meowing so loudly I thought the neighbors could hear her. When I took the turkey out of the oven, she would wait by my side as I carved it and beg for a piece. Occasionally, she hit the turkey jackpot because a piece would fall to the floor. And it didn't matter if the piece was quite large; she would dive right in and eat away.

If Clio liked turkey and chicken, she absolutely loved tuna. In fact, Clio could be sound asleep and snoring in the farthest room from the kitchen, but if someone even quietly opened a can of tuna, she would appear immediately, meowing loudly, begging for tuna and tuna juice. I probably gave her way too much tuna during her lifetime, but she seemed to live for it. In fact, she even knew the word *tuna* and what it meant. And like with the opening of a can, she could be sound asleep and even the whisper of the word would wake her up and start her incessantly meowing.

When Clio suspected she had a vet appointment, she would hide, and no matter how long and hard we searched for her, we couldn't find her. She wouldn't come out when I yelled her name. However, when I uttered the word *tuna*, Clio would come running even at the risk of a visit to the vet. But when I said that word, I knew I had to produce it for her or pay a severe price. Usually her punishment was to wake me up at two or three in the morning, or right after I had fallen asleep for the night. Clio never forgot a tuna slight. To her, it was the ultimate sin. We decided that if there were no tuna in Heaven and Clio's other choice was Hell, she'd take the latter because an eternal life without tuna was not worth living.

Two years after Jeff and I were married, my mother moved in with us. In fact, my mother would never have given up her home and made that move had it not been for Clio. Prior to moving in permanently, my mother would spend the winters at our home. One particularly harsh winter seemed to linger well into March when my mother decided she needed to return home. I begged her to stay since I was worried about her being housebound. Despite my best efforts, her decision to return to her home seemed irreversible. Then it occurred to me to say to her, "Well, what will Clio do without you? She'll be so worried." To my surprise, the next morning when I walked into the dining room, I heard my mother say to Clio (who was on the table sharing my mother's breakfast), "Clio, I'm going to stay, but only because of you. And when Kathy's away, I'll give you some tuna." Whatever works. I was just glad that my mother decided to wait until the severe winter ended before going home. I'm sure Clio was glad too, because while I was at my office, she was eating the tuna she had conned from my mother.

When my mother finally moved in with us later that year, Clio's dreams came true. She probably thought she had won the daily tuna lottery (not to be confused with the semiannual turkey lottery at Thanksgiving and Christmas). Clio no longer had to wait for the winter months to receive all the food and treats she wanted—this now went on all year long. Although I told my mother not to feed Clio from the table, I knew that she did. I also knew that now that my mother was there, Clio and Dickens enjoyed lunch. My mother felt that it was unfair that the cats didn't receive three meals a day. Her favorite line was "Clio is hungry and needs a snack." I found out, too, that my mother would pour the entire bag of treats into a bowl instead of just giving them one or two at a time. She would also sneak Clio tuna on Sunday mornings while I was in the shower and she was in the kitchen reading the newspaper. Obviously, Clio was ecstatic about the whole situation. She was finally receiving the amount and type of food she rightfully deserved.

Initially, my husband didn't believe in feeding animals from the table. However, even he soon fell victim to Clio's wiles and abandoned this misguided belief. He didn't give her table scraps, but he relented by allowing her on the table and even objected when I tried to remove her and relocate her to another room. Clio would wait until Jeff took his eyes off his food, then extend her paw and take something off his plate. She also seemed to really like the iced tea he made for us at dinner, and she would put her head into one of our glasses and drink.

One of my friends told me that I could easily break her of the bad habit of jumping on the table by spraying her with water when she attempted to get up there. I tried that once, and Clio simply sat there on the table leering at me while I emptied the spray bottle on her. I'm sure it works on some cats, but not Clio. I also tried startling her by shaking pennies in a can to stop her from jumping on the table. Again, I'm sure it works on some cats . . .

Nothing would come between Clio and her tuna, turkey, or chicken. She had several enablers in the house, and she thoroughly enjoyed taking advantage of every single one of them. Yes, Clio's table manners were truly appalling and her appetite endless. Yet this just endeared her to us more as her antics with food provided endless entertainment for my husband, my mother, and me, and brought us closer together. After all, even the best therapists have a few bad habits and their own obsessions.

# 9

# Knockin' Around
# the Christmas Tree

*To have a cat is to be forever entertained. No other crea-*
*ture is so affectionate and endearingly playful; yet cool,*
*calm, and self-possessed. It is impossible to keep a straight*
*face in the presence of one or more kittens.*

—CYNTHIA E. VARNADO

NOT ONLY DID CLIO'S EATING HABITS AMUSE US, BUT SPENDING
the holidays with her and Dickens provided us with inexpensive entertainment and helped us bond as a family. In fact, my first Christmas
with Clio made me feel the magic of the holiday season again. As a child,
I had enjoyed Christmas, but the holiday was a grim reminder that two
months before my eighth birthday my father died. The first Christmas
after his passing, relatives came to our home with presents to try to
make me feel better. It helped, but that feeling didn't last long, especially
since after that Christmas we rarely saw many of those relatives again.

My mother didn't have the money to buy expensive presents or to
have an elaborate Christmas celebration. Our Christmases were stark.
Although we enjoyed decorating our small, hand-me-down aluminum
tree (out of date even before we received it), we usually exchanged
only one or two gifts, almost always something we needed. Our tomcat, Lisa, did provide comic relief during the holidays, occasionally

knocking over the lightweight Christmas tree or playing with my mother's prized decorations from Europe. Yet it seemed that while others went to bed on Christmas Eve with thoughts of sugarplums dancing in their heads, I went to sleep hoping my mother had bought the right size white cotton underwear since it was always embarrassing to return underwear that didn't fit.

Nonetheless, I still enjoyed Christmas because I had two weeks off from school, and my mother went to great effort to make a variety of Hungarian pastries. My favorite treat was nut kifles, which required almost a full day to make and a lot of expensive ingredients. Because of the amount of work and money that went into making these cookies, she would hide them and then dole out one or two daily. Not having these cookies all the time made them taste even better, and I appreciated my daily allotment. Occasionally, my mother would surprise me with a gift of something I really wanted. Her excitement in giving me one of those gifts (like the record player I received one Christmas) was so contagious that it made the holiday even more special.

"Open it! Open it!" she would implore. "It's something you really wanted. Open it!" However, there was always the sadness that prevailed because my father was not there to watch me open presents or enjoy a nut kifle with us.

❧

In my first marriage, I told my husband, Alex, about how sad I would sometimes feel at Christmas, and how for the most part the few gifts I received were necessities and not surprises. At first, he tried to surprise me with gifts at Christmas to make me feel better. However, the good times didn't last long, and I soon realized that even though we didn't have much, the Christmases with my mother were at least full of love.

During the holidays, Alex and I would travel to either my mother's home or his dysfunctional parents' home. He often told me how he never remembered a Christmas without his parents fighting, and every Christmas after our first one together, it seemed like he would go out of his way to pick a fight with me to repeat his own personal history. Then after forty-five years of marriage, his parents decided to divorce.

As luck would have it, the year they filed for divorce, we spent Christmas with them. His father, claiming that he had to watch his money, turned the heat in the house down to fifty degrees, and their old furnace had trouble heating the house even to that temperature, given that the outside temperature was well below zero. There also were no presents that year from his parents because they were too caught up in their own drama. The entire week we spent with them was miserable. We felt obliged to listen to their "he said, she said" diatribes as they tried to convince us to take sides. I decided I would not take a side since I believed that they should have split up long before then.

After that Christmas with my in-laws and the one that followed, I was absolutely convinced that my husband was trying to make Christmas as miserable for me as it had been for him. His next-to-last attempt to ruin my favorite holiday came on Christmas Day during our fifteenth year of marriage. After I opened my one present from him (a bottle of bath oil), he revealed his affair and informed me that he no longer loved me. Later that day, I found out about the expensive ring he had bought his girlfriend. This made me long for the sincere gift of white cotton underwear from my mother. At least she hadn't bought me underwear and some other kid a shiny new bike while announcing on Christmas Day that she preferred the other kid to me.

One year later, Alex had the divorce papers delivered to me on Christmas Eve. Yet this final, and futile, attempt to ruin the holidays for me was unsuccessful. I had already decided to make every effort to enjoy my first Christmas with Clio. I filled the house with lights and all sorts of decorations and put up a large artificial Christmas tree (not the aluminum kind—although they were back in style—but a nice-looking green one). But having Clio is what made it truly fun. Little did I know then that the holidays to come spent with Clio, Dickens, and my mother would give me so many opportunities to remember that, as a child, receiving only a few presents yet plenty of love from my mother and a cat was not a bad way to spend Christmas.

Clio was fascinated by the large artificial tree I put up in the living room. It had to be assembled branch by branch, and Clio was right there helping with each branch and ornament. Once it was finished, she climbed the six-foot tree and hid in the branches. It was as if she knew that if I tried to extricate her, the ornaments would be sacrificed.

Over the years my mother enjoyed watching the cats work to undecorate the tree as I worked to decorate it, and keep it decorated. Dickens had not yet come into my life that first year, but the cat-in-tree tradition was eventually passed to him. At first Dickens stayed out of the tree, but I'm sure that when I was at the office, Clio taught him the ropes. In fact, Clio would often leave him in the tree so I would think that he was the guilty party, or I would come home and find them both deeply embedded in it.

When Clio wasn't in the tree, she was sitting on the small chair near it, perched over the arm and occasionally stretching out a paw to liberate an ornament from its branch. She also loved to sit under the tree and quietly undecorate the gifts by removing bows, tearing the wrapping paper, and pulling tissue paper out of the gift bags. And she would find her gifts (usually catnip toys) and proceed to unwrap them to sneak a peek. Above all, Clio's favorite activity was sleeping under the tree, and she and Dickens would jockey for a position among the presents.

A funny poem appeared on the Internet several years ago that reminded me of my Christmas tree after Clio and Dickens got hold of it.

CATS' TWELVE DAYS OF CHRISTMAS

*On the twelfth day of Christmas, I looked at my poor tree*

*12 cats a-climbing*

*11 broken branches*

*10 tinsel hairballs*

*9 chewed-through light strings*

*8 shattered ornaments*

*7 half-dead rodents*

*6 fallen angels*

*5 shredded gifts*

*4 males a-spraying*

*3 missing Wise Men*

*2 mangled garlands*

*And my 12 cats laughing at me.*

When it was time to take the tree down, I had to disassemble it branch by branch, and Clio and Dickens would huddle under the remaining branches looking sad. What a sorry sight. It was as if they were saying, "Please, please don't take down our tree. You won't let us out, so let us enjoy the outdoors indoors." Several years after we were married, Jeff and I bought a bag for the tree so we could more easily store it in the attic. However, before we took that bag up the stairs, we would have to check it because occasionally Clio would crawl inside. There was no way she was giving up on the tree just yet.

We eventually renovated our living room and put in a window seat near our front picture window in the exact spot where I had always placed the Christmas tree. The loss of floor space by the front window meant that we had to buy a smaller tree for a new location. Clio and Dickens weren't too happy about this. Soon, however, they discovered that the new location was much better for their covert purposes. Since the tree was now in a corner near the large fireplace hearth, it was virtually impossible for us to get them out of it, or even out from under it, without injuring ourselves or knocking it over and breaking the ornaments.

Another Christmas favorite of Clio's was the Department 56 Snow Village Jeff and I set up every Christmas on our hearth. Clio loved the village and would walk through it, knocking down plastic trees and ceramic people. Dickens would occasionally join in, and we always joked that it was as if giant cats were invading the village. Although Dickens was twice the size of Clio, amazingly he never knocked anything over. Clio could be very graceful, but something tells me she enjoyed knocking things over in the Christmas village.

Opening the gifts for the cats was always fun. In fact, it was more fun for us to watch the cats open their presents than it was to open our own (with their help of course). No matter what I purchased for Clio or Dickens, and many times they got the same thing, Clio would try to take Dickens's toy and Dickens would try to take hers. It was a whole new twist on holiday family feuds. After the fight, both would pass out from an "overdose" of catnip. However, the best Christmas gifts weren't the ones we bought. They were the boxes and tissue paper that our gifts came in. It would be months before I could throw away a tattered dress or shirt box with tissue paper. They never quite blended in with the living room decor, but when I tried to throw one away, Clio would run after me, begging me to keep it. And of course my mother would admonish, "Don't throw that away. Clio loves it."

One popular cat Christmas present was a laser pointer. Clio and Dickens would relentlessly follow the red dot, even attempting to chase it up a wall. We called the red dot a laser bug, and they would look around the house for hours, long after we'd put the toy away, wondering what had happened to that bug.

Except for the laser pointer, Clio and Dickens weren't into technology. One of the worst presents I bought them was a battery-powered mouse. They liked the mouse in the package, but when I placed it on the floor and turned it on, Dickens jumped backward and landed on my mother's lap—which scared him for a second time and almost caused my mother to have a heart attack. Once we recovered from the surprise, my mother and I laughed about it for hours.

Clio loved to pose for holiday photos. She would do anything for attention and a good photo, even allow us to dress her up with reindeer antlers or a crazy Christmas hat. Dickens, too, would wear Christmas hats and antlers, but I had to move quickly to get a good photo before he would take off running, trying to extricate himself from the festive headgear.

Whatever their antics during the holidays, Clio and Dickens put a smile on my face so I could once again enjoy Christmas. Indeed, the holidays were saved thanks to these two rescue cats, and my husband, who learned to appreciate Christmas with cats and a rather eccentric mother-in-law.

# *10*

# Clio, the Survivor

*Cats, as you know, are quite impervious to threats.*
—CONNIE WILLIS

AS I MENTIONED EARLIER, FOOD, HOLIDAYS, AND CATS ALWAYS brought our small family together. Those three things also brought me closer to Jeff, but it was the cats, and especially Clio, who helped strengthen our marriage. When we met, Jeff was a dog person who had never had a cat, and Clio's first goal was to convert him to a cat person. Ultimately, it was her many idiosyncrasies that endeared her to him and convinced him that he liked cats.

If living with two cats was not enough of a challenge, two years after we were married, my mother moved in with us. Jeff and I were faced with selling her home, packing all her belongings, moving her into our home, and adjusting to our new living arrangement. Then not long after my mother moved in, adversity struck our beloved Clio. She developed cancer.

🐾

Clio had a knack for getting into trouble and therefore was no stranger to Dr. Dave and his staff, or to the staff at the emergency vet clinic. For example, several months before I met Jeff, I came home from work one day to freshen up before going out with my board members, who were in town for a meeting. When I walked in the house, I found Clio lying on the floor howling and writing in pain. My heart sank.

"Clio! Clio! What's wrong with you?" I yelled as if I expected a cat to answer me.

My first thought was that this precious little cat who meant the world to me may have had a stroke, and I had grown to love her so much that I couldn't imagine a life without her. Panicked, I called the emergency vet clinic (it was after Dr. Dave's normal hours) and was told to bring her in immediately. I then called one of my board members to let them know I would be late since I had to take my cat to the vet. They probably thought I was crazy, but I didn't care.

The vet examined her but couldn't find anything wrong. He said that more blood tests were necessary and it would be best if I left her overnight. Worried that they would find something seriously wrong, I implored: "What could be wrong with her? Could it be fatal? Did she have a stroke? Please tell me she'll be okay."

Before the vet had a chance to calm me down and tell me not to jump to any conclusions before the tests were completed, Clio leaped off the examining table and started running around the room. That's when we noticed her limp. The vet x-rayed her hind leg and returned to tell me she had pulled ligaments in her knee. Who knew cats had knees? He then taped her up with hot-pink tape and sent her home, telling me that I probably should take her to my regular vet when he got in the next day (which I did).

Dr. Dave decided that it would be best not to operate to repair the ligaments because her heart murmur had persisted after kittenhood, and any nonessential surgery was not worth the risk. I conjectured that Clio had injured herself by suddenly jumping or falling off something she wasn't supposed to be on when I came home a bit early and surprised her.

This incident was not the only health scare for Clio. I mentioned earlier that she pulled out her stitches after she was spayed. That was a Saturday afternoon spent in the emergency animal clinic. Then one Easter she ate part of a hyacinth that I had placed high on a shelf in my kitchen. (This is when I learned that there was practically no surface in the house too high for her to reach.) Clio began to have severe diarrhea. I was unaware that she had gotten to the hyacinth until, fortunately and coincidentally, I moved the plant to find something else on the shelf and noticed that the leaves and flowers had been chewed. Once again we had to pay a visit to the emergency vet clinic for treatment.

Then there was the time she chewed on the silk ivy in a planter on the divider that separated the living and dining rooms and the metal end of a branch got stuck in her teeth. For several minutes we thought we would be making another trip to the emergency clinic, but fortunately we were able to extricate it, thankful that the metal wire wasn't implanted in her tongue.

Clio knew no fear and could get herself into trouble in no time, but she had always managed to survive. That survival instinct helped her when she developed cancer. Fortunately, Jeff was in my life to help me face her diagnosis and the possibility of losing my sweet little Clio.

🐾

Clio's cancer journey began shortly after I adopted Dickens (while I was still single), when I noticed a black spot on her eye. I immediately called Dr. Dave, who told me it probably was nothing but I should bring her in just to be safe. I took her to the vet clinic, and Dr. Dave said it was melanin, or discoloration of the eye. It was just a freckle, but he told me that I should watch it and if it got bigger, I might consider going to a cat ophthalmologist because sometimes these spots can turn into melanoma. A cat ophthalmologist? He had to be joking, but he wasn't.

As the year wore on, I noticed the spot was beginning to enlarge, so I decided to take her to Dr. Vestre, a well-known cat ophthalmologist. Over several years, Dr. Vestre meticulously watched this spot as it slowly grew. Eventually, the spot dispersed on the iris, and her beautiful green eye turned dark brown. Yet even after that, there was no evidence that it had turned to melanoma.

After I married Jeff, we continued to monitor Clio's eye condition. Every three months, I would put Clio in the pet carrier and take her to the eye doctor. This generated some interesting conversation at work since the ophthalmologist would call my office to remind me of Clio's appointment. When I was busy, the receptionist would take a message. The first time the ophthalmologist called, the receptionist came to me with a rather bewildered look on her face and said, "Your cat's eye doctor called you. I think it may have been a prank call." "I filled her in on the details, and after that she enjoyed paging me on the office intercom when Dr. Vestre's office called, saying, "Kathy, line one. Your cat's eye doctor is trying to reach you." Immediately I would hear the staff chuckling.

Clio was indeed a survivor, but it certainly wasn't because she was a good patient. Getting her into the carrier was always an adventure. One time we tried a relaxant prescribed by Dr. Dave. Clio promptly fell asleep, but the moment I brought the carrier in from the garage, she got an adrenaline rush. Even when drugged, she put up quite a fight. For that reason, on all future vet visits I would sneak the carrier in the house the night before and place it in the small shower stall in the bathroom with the open side up while my husband distracted her with tuna. The carrier barely fit in that stall because we had to buy a dog-sized one so she couldn't spread her stiffened back legs over the opening, preventing us from getting her in without breaking her legs. With a bigger carrier we had room to wrap her in a towel and put her in backward, although she still put up a great struggle, making it difficult for us to confine her. This was a case of having one chance to kiss the pig. If she got away, we wouldn't be able to find her in time to make it to the appointment.

Clio lived with the spot on her eye for five years, and during that period my husband and I became experts at cat wrestling. As frustrated as I would get with Clio and her antics to avoid the vet, I never got angry with her because I knew that any one of these visits could result in the diagnosis I didn't want to hear—that the spot had turned to melanoma and the eye would have to be removed if we wanted to save her life. In the spring of that year, Dr. Vestre told me just that.

"The spot is turning to melanoma and moving dangerously close to her brain. Her eye has to come out immediately," he said.

"Immediately?" I said. "But . . . a few months ago, it was fine. And she has such beautiful green eyes."

"These spots change rapidly. She'll live a long, happy life as a one-eyed cat. If we do nothing, the cancer will spread to her brain, and she'll be dead in a few months."

"Okay . . . I certainly don't want to lose her."

Clio made it through the surgery just fine, but when we went to pick her up that evening, she looked so pitiful. Dr. Vestre had done a good job of covering the eye socket with her gray fur, but her face was terribly swollen. However, since her eye had darkened so much in recent years, having it gone wasn't noticeable to us from a distance.

We brought our sweet Clio home, and I lay down on the couch. After a long sleepless night and a stressful day of worrying about whether her surgery would go well and that the cancer had spread, I started to cry for her, but before I knew it, she was on top of me, licking my face and purring loudly. She was the one who needed comfort, and yet she was comforting me.

I just hoped they were able to remove all the cancer and she would be able to live a full life.

The next day, we had planned to take my mother and my father-in-law's wife to dinner to celebrate their mutual birthday. Jeff's sister, father, and his father's wife came to our house, then we all went out to dinner. Clio had spent most of the day sleeping, and she raised her head just slightly when Jeff's family arrived. We quickly left for dinner so Clio could rest.

After dinner, everyone came back to our house for a shared birthday cake. To Clio, our return signaled that it was entertainment time since, in her mind, the day following surgery was no different from any other occasion when Jeff's family came over. Clio always showed off for guests and loved being the center of attention. And even though she had what equated to a fairly major surgery for a person, this was showtime for her, and she wasn't about to let this little eye-removal incident stand in her way. She batted around her glitter ball and then went over to the couch, looked back at everyone, tucked her head between her front paws, and did one of her famous somersaults—of course making sure that everyone was looking at her since she was the most beautiful and talented cat in the world and that's why everyone had come to her house. She obviously figured that since people were laughing and pointing at her, she would do another somersault, and then another.

The next morning, I found Clio in her bed with her head firmly pressed against the side as if to say, "Leave me alone—I have a splitting headache." I'm not sure whether cats get headaches, but I would imagine she had severe pain from the surgery, and all those somersaults could not have helped. I decided that it was time to give her a quarter of a baby aspirin, which Dr. Vestre had been recommended for pain.

Getting a pill down Clio's throat was always a challenge. I didn't know cats could spit and really don't think most of them can, but Clio learned how to spit and went for distance. When we put an aspirin down her throat, she'd spit it across the room—a good ten feet away. I also had to give her an antibiotic and learned that cats can snort fluid through their noses. I gave her the antibiotic in liquid form just like the vet told us: "It's easy. Just open her mouth, put the dropper filled with the antibiotic near the back of her tongue, and squeeze. The medicine will go down her throat without any trouble." Well, maybe with other cats ... When I squeezed the pink fluid out of the dropper in the back of Clio's throat, it came out of her nose. She had refused to swallow and somehow inhaled it. Clio would do anything to avoid taking medicine, but this little incident probably made veterinary medical history.

Fortunately we had caught Clio's eye cancer in time. After thorough analysis in a San Francisco veterinary pathology lab, Clio's eye showed no sign that the cancer had spread. We were delighted when we received the call giving her a clean bill of health, and to learn that cats don't have depth perception problems even if an eye is removed. After her eye healed and the stitches were removed, Clio went back to her normal life: continuing her complicated relationship with Dickens, doing somersaults, playing with her glitter balls at three in the morning, chasing flies endlessly at all hours of the night, and jumping up on everything.

The surgery not only saved her life, but it seemed to give her even more confidence in her abilities. If I were in the same situation and had lost an eye, I would have been a basket case and worried about not only how I looked but what other people thought of me. But not Clio.

The removal of her eye only made her more distinctive and unique. To her, it didn't matter that she had only one eye. She had a great sense of self-worth—she was still beautiful, talented, and intelligent. How could the loss of an eye change that?

Slowly but surely as Clio returned to her normal routine and regained her cattitude, I realized that my marriage to Jeff had grown stronger, as had my relationship with my mother. Moreover, my self-confidence and self-esteem continued to grow as I recognized that a person's true beauty is internal, not external. I also began to believe that God or a higher being was looking after Clio and me. He didn't take Clio from me, and despite losing an eye, she was still a spunky, self-confident, and loving cat. And it was her bout with cancer that would bring my husband and me closer together and further improve the relationship I had with my mother. It also taught us to persevere no matter how difficult the obstacles. Consequently, when I had a cancer scare a few years later, thoughts of Clio's bravery gave me the courage and hope to face the situation.

# 11

# Beating the Odds

*There are no ordinary cats.*
—COLETTE

CLIO WAS A SURVIVOR AND MANAGED TO SURVIVE, AND EVEN thrive, after a successful surgery for eye cancer. A few years later, however, she faced a second, more serious bout with cancer that once again drew our small family together and made Clio an extraordinary cat.

This new cancer ordeal began shortly after I returned from a long business trip. Totally exhausted after several fourteen-hour days on my feet, I decided to take a nap. Always upon my return from traveling, Clio would seek me out to either sit on my lap or curl up next to me. Her presence by my side helped me to relax, especially once she started to purr. This time was no different. Clio snuggled up next to me and started purring loudly. I began to pet her and as I moved my hand over her hind leg, I was startled when I felt what I thought was a lump. *How could that be?* I thought. *I just took her to the vet a few weeks ago for her annual checkup and vaccinations and she was fine.* Clio tried to wiggle away from me as I held her down to determine whether this was a lump. And it was—a hard, jagged lump. My hand froze in place as a sinking feeling came over me. I knew that in humans any lump that is hard and jagged is never good.

Despite being exhausted to the point of almost collapsing, I called our vet, Dr. Dave. Vicky, his vet tech, answered the phone. Given Clio's propensity to get into trouble that necessitated veterinary care and her bout with eye cancer, Vicky recognized my voice since I had called their office so many times. She also usually surmised that I was calling about Clio instead of Dickens.

"Hi, Vicky."

"Hi, Kathy. What's up with Clio?"

"I was just petting her, and I noticed a hard lump in her hind leg."

"Let me have you talk to Dr. Dave."

When Dr. Dave answered, I repeated what I had told Vicky and added, "I'm not sure if it's anything . . ."

"Is it the leg where she received the leukemia vaccine?"

"Yes, I think so."

"You need to bring her in immediately."

"Could it be cancer?"

"I won't know until I examine her. Go ahead and bring her in right now, and I'll see what it is. It's probably nothing, but I need to see her."

We quickly wrestled Clio into her carrier and drove her to the vet clinic. Dr. Dave examined the lump manually and said that it had to come out since it most likely was cancer. My first thought was that the eye cancer had spread, but this was a different type of cancer, and I was assured that the two were not related.

Dr. Dave kept Clio overnight so he could operate on her the next day. As usual, she recovered from the surgery quickly. I brought her home the afternoon of the surgery, and as soon as the effects of the anesthetic wore off, she was running around the house.

A few days after the surgery, Dr. Dave called with the bad news. The lump was proliferative fibrosarcoma, an extremely aggressive form of cancer. Although Dr. Dave had removed the tumor as well as wide margins around it, this type of cancer had an 80 percent chance of recurrence and was likely to metastasize. He noted that it was most likely caused by the feline leukemia vaccine. *Great. By trying to be a good pet parent, I had accidentally inflicted more pain on Clio.* Dr. Dave noted that less than one-tenth of 1 percent of cats develop cancer from the vaccine, the same percentage that gets eye cancer. Yet, she got cancer twice. I figured that the chance of getting both types of cancers was phenomenally small—about the same as for me winning the lottery—but Clio played the odds. My husband, Jeff, and I often wondered and asked each other, "If Clio purchased a lottery ticket, would she win millions?"

I asked Dr. Dave if we should follow up with radiation therapy or chemotherapy, but he noted that this type of treatment was unavailable where we lived. He told us, however, that there was a cat oncologist four hours away in another state, and if we wanted, he would call and set up an appointment.

Since the oncologist's vet specialty was so rare, it was hard to get an appointment. The earliest we could get one was slightly over a month away, which turned out to be immediately after Christmas. The thought of driving four hours in a possible snowstorm with a howling cat was not pleasant, but I wanted to do everything I could to save Clio's life. She was a survivor, and I knew she could survive this bout of cancer too. Although still not religious, I asked God to spare my poor little Clio. However, the skeptic in me didn't prevent me from wondering whether Clio had been sent to me as a cruel joke. She had done so much for me, but was this too good to be true? Was God going to take her from me as he had taken my father and my dog when I was a child?

Fortunately, it did not snow on the day of Clio's appointment, although the weather did match our mood. It was forty degrees, with rain coming down in torrents. The windshield wipers had difficulty keeping up, which made it hard to see and added to our growing sense of despair about our mission. Luckily for us, Clio only howled for the first fifteen minutes of the four-hour trip to the oncologist's office and then stopped when she realized we weren't going to Dr. Dave's. Of course she didn't know we were taking her to another veterinarian. It seemed to be an exciting adventure for her. I could see her trying to peer out all sides of the carrier.

The rain was so heavy and wind so gusty that at times I thought we should be traveling by boat. Jeff and I tried to imagine what was going through Clio's mind and decided that given her love of tuna, she may be thinking we were in a tuna fishing boat, and soon we would stop to cast our line and share our catch with her. Our imaginary scenarios helped break the tension we both felt as we continued the journey out of state to find out what, if anything, we could do to save our sweet little Clio.

We finally arrived at the oncologist's office and took Clio inside. She immediately realized that she was in a vet's office and started howling. Fortunately for the other patients, we were soon ushered into the examining room. When the oncologist came in, Clio tried to hide under the small towel in her carrier, barely big enough to cover her head. Once the doctor got Clio out of her carrier, she looked her over, examined the area near the incision, and reviewed the medical and lab reports Dr. Dave had given us. Then she noted, "Here's an article about proliferative fibrosarcoma. There isn't much research on this type of cancer. It's extremely rare for a cat to get cancer from the leukemia vaccine."

"Yes, our vet told us how rare it is," I said.

"The problem is that this form of sarcoma in cats is so rare that we don't have a lot of data on it. From what we have, the prognosis is not good. However, I do think there is some good news for Clio and you. The tumor was low in her leg—not near the hip. If we remove her leg at the hip, there's a very good chance the cancer won't spread, and she'll live."

I was shocked. "What??? Remove her entire hind leg. But our vet said he removed all the cancer, and there were clean margins. Shouldn't we do chemo instead?"

"Yes, he did, but in this type of cancer, it's not unusual that a few cells get into the scar tissue and spread from there. Chemo won't help. But by removing her leg at the hip, it's very likely that the cancer will not return."

"Okay," I said. "I guess we should have her leg amputated, but are you sure she will be able to get around?"

"Animals are very adaptable, and I can tell Clio is a survivor. She may look a little odd, and you may have the only one-eyed, three-legged cat in the world, but it won't matter to her, and I don't think that it will matter to you, either."

"If that is her only hope, then let's go ahead with the surgery," I said reluctantly.

We decided to have Dr. Dave perform the amputation rather than have it done out of state. While we were still in the office, the oncologist called Dr. Dave to make sure he had the equipment to do the surgery and to give him more specific instructions. However, before she left to call him, she asked if Clio needed anything (never mind that Jeff and I had driven for four hours and were both in desperate need of a bathroom and some water). Clio had a definite knack for looking pitiful. We indicated that she might need to use the litter box and perhaps was thirsty.

The vet tech gave Clio what looked like a shoe box lid filled with litter and a small container of water, as well as a little dry food. Clio's response was to crawl under the small towel in her carrier. She probably thought this was a strange, strange hotel, and certainly the staff needed a lesson in feline hospitality. Yet, I think she believed that she dodged a bullet because no one stuck a needle in her or removed anything. If only she knew of our plans . . .

Before we left, we scheduled an appointment with Dr. Dave to perform the surgery. Then we packed up Clio and headed home. It poured rain all the way home, again matching our mood. Any surgery on Clio was risky because of her heart murmur, so during our car ride back home I asked Jeff whether he thought we were doing the right thing.

"If we want Clio to live, we are doing the right thing," he said. "If we do nothing, the cancer will come back, which means another surgery and more pain. And eventually, they won't be able to operate on her, and then it could be very painful for her. Clio's a survivor."

"But will she be able to walk on three legs?"

"How long did it take her to adjust to one eye?"

"Not very long."

"That's my point exactly," Jeff said. "She'll adjust."

"But she has a heart murmur."

"Yes, but she's made it through other surgeries."

"Do you think she wants to live?" I asked. "Even if it means it will be more difficult for her to get around? And we are subjecting her to more pain? This isn't just about us wanting her to live, is it? Are we being selfish?"

"Well, of course we want her to live. And yes, she wants to live. I'm sure she doesn't want Dickens getting all her food, and she especially doesn't want him to get all the tuna."

"You're right. Clio wants to live, and this is the best thing for her. She'll make it through this too. I'm sure she will," I said, doubting my words the minute they came out of my mouth.

The day of Clio's surgery came all too fast, and it was difficult in the days leading up to the procedure to think about it and to listen to my mother, whose bond with Clio had grown stronger since she moved in with us. My mother kept questioning us on whether this was fair to her little friend (which, of course, I had already asked myself). However, even more difficult was denying Clio food and drink after midnight the day of the surgery.

Clio didn't care about drinking, but she was unbearable when we withheld food from her. Feeding Dickens without feeding her was asking for a lot of trouble. How dare we feed her archrival and not her. When Clio was hungry (which seemed to be most of the time), she was relentless in her pursuit of food. The gentle meows and cute looks turned to bloodcurdling screeches and an evil look. Yes, I know cats are not known for their expressive faces, but Clio was different. One look at her and you knew immediately whether she was happy or upset, and on the day of the surgery anyone, cat person or not, would have recognized the depth of Clio's anger.

We awoke early that dreaded morning to take Clio to the vet. The minute we dropped her off, we were sick to our stomachs. I couldn't go to work and spent most of the morning pacing back and forth awaiting word from Dr. Dave that Clio had made it through the surgery. What if she died of a heart murmur? What if the tests were wrong and her kidneys failed to flush the anesthesia out of her system? The what ifs kept coming. I'm surprised my pacing didn't wear out the carpet. Then the phone rang—it was Dr. Dave.

My heart stopped. "Is Clio all right?" I asked. "Did something happen to her?"

"Don't worry," Dr. Dave said. "Clio made it through the surgery fine and is in recovery. In fact, she's doing quite well. I know how she hates staying at the vet clinic overnight, so if she continues to improve, you can take her home in one of our cages. Just keep her in the cage, away from Dickens. Vicky will call you if she continues to improve, and you can pick her up."

"Thank you. Thank you."

Before hanging up, Dr. Dave noted that Clio's leg was sent off to a pathology lab in Wisconsin. (Clio's body parts were now scattered across the United States—her eye was in San Francisco and now her leg in Wisconsin.) He said it would be several weeks before they had the results but noted that, visually, everything looked good. We were extremely happy with the news.

By midafternoon, Vicky called and said I could pick up Clio. I arrived at the vet clinic at a quarter to five, and together, Vicky and I loaded the cage with Clio into my MINI Cooper. The cage barely fit, but we managed to get it into the back of the car.

When we got home at about ten after five, I struggled to get the cage out of the car. Once inside, I set the cage on the kitchen floor and went back to the garage to close the hatchback. To my surprise, when I came back into the kitchen, I found Dickens looking into the cage and Clio hopping around inside hissing at him. Right away I noticed that she had managed to pull off her bandages and feared that she would pull out her stitches. Bringing Clio home so soon after the surgery was a mistake. I immediately called Vicky.

"Hello, Vicky. This is Kathy. I just got home with Clio, and she's already pulled off her bandages and is standing up in the cage."

"*Whaat?* She pulled off all the bandages and is standing up?"

"Yes, and she's hissing at Dickens."

"Really?"

"Yes, really."

"You need to bring her back immediately. I have to leave in about an hour. Can you get her back here quickly? Also, everyone's left the clinic, so can you help me get the bandages back on?"

"Sure. I'll leave right now, and I can stay with her."

"And you realize she will need to stay overnight at the clinic."

"Yes, I know. It will be best for her," I said as I hung up the phone, knowing that I would rather have her home with us.

Just as I had worked up a sweat struggling to put the cage back into my car, my husband pulled into the drive, looking puzzled. But before he could ask, I said to him, "I don't have time to explain. I'll tell you all about this on the way to the vet. Just get in the car!"

In my mind, I could imagine Clio saying, "Wait a minute . . . You aren't taking me back to the vet, are you? Sorry about pulling off the bandages. Well, actually, I'm not sorry. They were really constraining my movement, and I'm doing just fine."

Despite Clio's loud protestations about being returned to the vet, I drove the MINI Cooper like I'd stolen it.

When we arrived at the clinic and unloaded the cage, Vicky looked in at Clio and said, "How in the world did she do this?"

Although Vicky was amazed at Clio's ability to be up hopping around so quickly, we weren't. Clio was just being Clio. Unfortunately, she had to stay at the vet not only that night but for the rest of the week. Had Clio done what she was supposed to do, she could have spent the week at home, but being a good patient just wasn't in her DNA.

# 12

# Playing the Sympathy Card

*Anyone who believes what a cat tells him
deserves all he gets.*    —NEIL GAIMAN

ON FRIDAY, WE FINALLY WERE ABLE TO RETRIEVE CLIO FROM
Dr. Dave's after the amputation of her hind leg. Because her incision
was seeping, we had to cover the living room floor with towels. We
also had to confine her to the dining and living room area because
those were the rooms where she could do the least damage to herself.

The surgery didn't affect Clio's appetite. She was just as hungry
as ever, and now because she had difficulty walking, she received additional servings of tuna delivered via "room service"—that is, we
took her food to wherever she was and put it in front of her because
it seemed cruel to make her hop all the way to her food bowl in the
kitchen. Clio soon learned that room service was a cool idea. She didn't
even have to go to the kitchen for food. Moreover, we gave her all the
tuna she wanted. She just needed to meow loudly, and we would retrieve the food and place it in front of her. As with all habits that are
bad, Clio completely embraced this new practice.

Using the litter box wasn't easy for Clio at first. She had trouble getting in, and then trouble standing up. I think after watching her move-
ments, Dickens felt that Clio was a "dead cat walking." He started
hissing at her and taking advantage of her by pushing her away from

her food. Dickens apparently didn't think she was long for this world. Nothing could have been further from the truth, and I knew that once Clio recovered, this three-legged, one-eyed cat was going to make him regret his decision. And she did.

Slowly but surely, Clio recovered from the surgery and learned how to walk—or more accurately, hop—on three legs. It was amazing how rapidly she adapted and how quickly she realized that her new disability had its advantages. Clio now had a new gig—gaining sympathy—and it was going to last a long time. However, I was so thankful she was going to live that I didn't care that she was using this recent medical crisis to her own advantage.

Jeff's father called the day after Clio's surgery while Jeff was in bed with a bad case of the flu. I answered the phone and let him know that Jeff was sick.

"I didn't call to talk to Jeff," his father said. "I called about Clio. Is she okay? Is she? We are really worried about her."

I don't think he even heard me tell him that Jeff was ill.

Even our neighbors, who were die-hard dog people, called to ask about her. Between relatives and friends, our telephone was ringing nonstop. Everyone was worried about Clio. Over her seven years of life, she had developed quite a fan club.

After a few weeks, Dr. Dave called with the results from the pathology lab in Wisconsin. The minute he said, "Hi, this is Dr. Dave," my heart stopped again. But this time the news was good, and Clio was given a clean bill of health. We were ecstatic. Although there were a few cancer cells in the scar tissue where the tumor had been removed, there was no evidence of cancer cells in the rest of the leg or hip. The prognosis was good, and I was extremely thankful that Clio would be in my life for years to come. Moreover, it made me believe that maybe God didn't hate me and actually listened to my prayers.

However, a clean bill of health from the vet didn't mean that Clio wasn't going to take full advantage of this near-death experience and continue to play the sympathy card. Although we had always tried (with little success) to keep her off the kitchen counter and table, we now would place her there because her "jumper" was broken. We put small footstools by the beds, the sofa, and chairs so she could easily get on the furniture. When our friends came over, she would look up at them, and without asking us, they would reach for the treats on the kitchen counter and give her one because she was "such a little trooper." My mother, who already gave Clio anything she wanted but previously would get angry when she jumped on the kitchen table (especially when my mother was eating), now would ask us to put her on the table. When Clio would grab something from her plate, instead of saying, "Get the cat off the table," she would ask, "Clio, are you hungry?"

I'd say, "Clio, stop licking her plate," and my mother would admonish, "Oh, she's not hurting anything. Don't yell at poor, sweet little Clio. She's endured so much, and she deserves a treat."

A few months after Clio's surgery, one of my credit cards was stolen. I called the bank and was told I had to report it to the police. When I called the police and asked for the nearest station, they said they would send an officer to our home. As the officer walked into the house, he saw Clio. His first words were "What happened to her? Is she happy?" Then when she meowed, he asked me if we had some treats he could give her. Here was a veteran police officer who probably took down many a criminal, including con artists, being conned by an eleven-pound, one-eyed, three-legged cat.

Clio continued to work the sympathy routine, especially when it came to jumping on the beds, tables, and counters. Granted, jumping from the floor to the counter was out of the question, but Clio had figured out how to jump up on almost everything else. Several months after the surgery, my cousin from Ohio came to visit, along with my aunt from Florida. In retrospect, I really think they came to see Clio and not me. After they arrived, we decided to go out to dinner. Since both my husband and I had MINI Coopers, we had to take two cars to the restaurant. I took my aunt, and my husband took my cousin.

Jeff returned from the restaurant first with my cousin and came in the house to find Clio curled up on her favorite living room chair. This was the same chair she would look at and then look at me as if to say, "Pick me up. I can't jump up there anymore." She looked up when they came in and, I am sure, determined that although they now knew she could jump, she still had me bamboozled. I came home about five minutes later and, as my husband tells it, the moment the garage door went up, she woke up, looked as if she'd seen a ghost, and quickly jumped off the chair, obviously not wanting me to catch her. When I walked into the living room, she was sitting on the floor by the chair, looking pitiful.

My aunt immediately said, "Oh, pick her up. She wants on the chair and can't jump."

Clio was indeed quite the con artist.

For several months after her surgery, we had to take Clio in for checkups and x-rays to make sure the cancer hadn't spread to her lungs. Before the amputation, it was almost impossible to get her in the oversized carrier without wrapping her in a towel and backing her in. Putting Clio in the carrier was always a two-person task because she would plant her stiffened hind legs on each side of the opening and then try to kick the carrier. I would wrap her in a towel to prevent that, but my husband always had to hold the carrier as I guided her in. But with only one hind leg, getting her in the carrier was now much easier. It didn't stop her from wiggling to try to get away, or from letting out bloodcurdling meows, but I was able to get her in by myself without the towel and without my husband supporting the carrier After several months of taking her to the vet on my own, my husband again asked, "Do you need help getting her to the vet?"

"No," I replied. "Without her hind leg, there's no way she can prevent me from placing her in the carrier. I'll be fine. Go on to work."

"Are you sure? Something tells me that she's figured out a way to outsmart us by now."

"I'm sure. Go on to work."

"Okay."

The night before, I had put the carrier in the shower stall so she wouldn't see it. After Jeff departed for work, I followed my morning routine by eating breakfast while watching the morning news, trying not to set off her sixth sense about the vet visit. By about seven thirty, Clio had fallen asleep on the bed, so I quickly picked her up and walked to the small bathroom. Unlike with the vet visits prior to her leg amputation, I decided not to wrap her in a towel since she didn't have two hind legs to straddle the carrier opening. It was unpleasant to hear her shrieking, but compared to previous vet visits, I thought this would be a piece of cake.

I opened the shower stall and tried to drop her in the carrier. Much to my surprise, Clio braced her remaining hind leg on one side of the opening and her tail on the other. Yes, her tail! I couldn't budge her. Her tail was as hard and strong as a rock. I had no idea that a cat's tail had muscles and could become sinewy. I had to pick her back up, find a towel, wrap her tightly in it, and then back her into the carrier. Rather shaken, I put the carrier in the car.

On the way to the vet clinic, I called my husband and said, "Guess what? You were right. Clio outsmarted me again. You won't believe what happened when I tried to put her in her carrier." Of course, he did believe it and only chuckled because he knew her all too well. Dr. Dave, though, looked puzzled when I told him about the incident. I'm sure he thought I was exaggerating—that is, until he turned around and bent down to look at her and she slapped him in the face with her tail. Then he believed me. In learning to walk again, Clio used her tail for balance and had developed strong muscles in it, so every time we went to the vet after that, I once again had to enlist the help of my husband to steady the carrier and guide her in.

I should have known that Clio would never make going to the vet easy. But what she did make easier was for me to realize that no matter how big the obstacles and no matter what the odds, we can persevere and not only survive but thrive. Clio continued to live life as she always had: eating tuna, romping, and chasing Dickens around the house. And despite having only three legs and one eye, she was able to jump up on most of our furniture and could put up quite a fight to avoid being placed in a pet carrier.

಄

A few years later, I went to the doctor for my annual checkup. During that visit I noted that I was experiencing more fatigue than usual. My doctor then observed that my neck was enlarged, and upon preliminary examination she told me there was a possibility of thyroid cancer. My heart sank because no one wants to hear the "C" word. I had witnessed my grandfather die a horrible death from cancer and had taken care of my mother when she had uterine cancer. Other relatives and friends, too, had developed cancer and died. If there was one thing in life I dreaded, it was a cancer diagnosis.

After the doctor visit and before I underwent several tests, I read up on thyroid cancer, and it seemed that many of the symptoms I was experiencing pointed to it. Mentally, I prepared myself for the worst. Fortunately, the tests showed that it was not cancer—just a goiter with benign nodules. However, before receiving this diagnosis, I had already decided that if it was cancer, I would fight it. After all, Clio had survived cancer twice, and the odds of beating it the second time were not good, so I would not let cancer get the best of me.

As I reflected on Clio's two bouts with cancer, I realized how much I had learned from her about resilience, determination, and self-esteem. She had overcome severe disabilities yet still maintained a high level of self-esteem and was adept at turning every disadvantage into an advantage. Quitting wasn't in her vocabulary. And from now on, it wasn't going to be in mine.

Clio had changed my outlook on life. I had overcome a lot—the loss of my father at a young age, growing up in poverty, being bullied at school to the point that it destroyed my self-esteem, and an abusive first marriage. Clio had overcome a lot too. Because of her triumph over cancer, Clio became very distinctive. Her two cancer surgeries left her with one eye, three legs, and additional doses of cattitude. Clio was indeed no ordinary cat and proud of it. Her looks and disabilities had no effect on her self-esteem, confidence, spunkiness, and love of me (and tuna).

Clio wasn't perfect, and I didn't need to be, either. At times she was clumsy and silly, but she was fine with that. This made me realize that maybe I should be content with who I am. There was no doubt that as difficult as Clio's recent tribulations were, my self-esteem was growing thanks to my one-eyed, three-legged therapist.

# 13

# Nothing to Fear but Fear Itself and a Cat Who Has No Fear

*The proverbial curiosity doesn't usually kill cats. The inquisitive feline has a knack of dodging death by a whisker. Cats are intrepid explorers and fearless acrobats. After all, a creature with nine lives can afford to take risks. According to* Brewer's Dictionary of Phrase and Fable *[1896], a cat is said to have nine lives because it is more tenacious of life than many animals.*

—JUSTINE HANKINS

"WHAT MATTERS MOST IS HOW YOU SEE YOURSELF" IS THE CAPtion to a popular image often seen on motivational posters. It features a yellow kitten who looks into a mirror and sees a lion. That poster could have easily featured Clio. Unlike Dickens, who was afraid of his own shadow, Clio feared absolutely nothing (except maybe a trip to the vet), and her self-confidence was off the charts.

Most of the time, Clio's fearlessness worked in her favor, but sometimes it got her into a lot of trouble, which again provided us with endless hours of entertainment. For example, Clio would play hard and wasn't afraid of getting hurt, and she always loved having an audience to witness her antics. A classic example was the "electric slide" she performed in the nook in our main bathroom. Clio liked to lie on her side on the bathroom floor, then, with her back foot firmly planted against one wall of the nook, she would push off and slide to the opposite wall. Usually she stopped short, but when she noticed us watching, she would push off too hard and slam her head hard into the wall. This did not stop her from doing it repeatedly.

She also would do a high-wire act on the narrow footboard at the end our bed. Instead of watching what she was doing, she would make sure we were focused on her, and in doing so walk right off the end of the bed and tumble to the floor. Nonchalantly, she would get up and look at us as if to say, "I meant to do that."

Yet nothing matched Clio's fearlessness when it came to taking on animals larger than herself. Dickens was twice her size and very muscular, but that never stopped Clio. Of course she had grown up with Dickens and probably convinced him at an early age that she was the stronger and fiercer of the two. However, Clio's fearlessness went beyond teasing her adoptive feline brother. Repeatedly she took on dogs, no matter how big or how fierce.

Clio's first encounter with a dog came when she was less than a year old. The family next door adopted a Labrador Retriever named Jessie. One day I took her over to meet Jessie, who immediately wagged her tail and looked interested, but Clio would have no part in befriending her. Instead, she hissed and swatted Jessie. She did the same to another neighbor's Labrador, Reggie, who was much more tolerant than Jessie and would back away any time he saw Clio.

Clio's early success at intimidating animals larger than herself served to encourage her. Our next-door neighbors' house was close to ours, and when Jessie was in the side yard by the kitchen and bedroom windows, Clio would sit in the window, hissing and taunting her. An electric fence kept Jessie in her yard, but Clio didn't realize that Jessie would break through the fence occasionally to pursue a squirrel or a chipmunk, or possibly a little gray-and-white cat she saw in our window.

One time when Jessie broke loose and her pet parents weren't home, we put her in our garage until they returned. At the time there was a defunct furnace vent in our laundry room. The laundry room was next to the interior garage wall, and the vent opened to the garage but was missing the cover, leaving a hole in the garage wall. The vent cover in the laundry room was still in place, but it wasn't fastened very tightly. Clio knew Jessie was in the garage, so she decided to put her nose up to the vent cover and taunt her. Jessie took the bait. She put her nose in the opening, started barking, and began to push against the inside vent cover so it would fall out and she could grab Clio. As Jessie managed to loosen the cover, Clio realized she had tweaked the tail of the tiger and ran to the bedroom farthest from the laundry room. She came out from under the bed two hours later, which was about an hour after the neighbors had retrieved poor Jessie.

My sister-in-law, Karen, had two dogs—J'aime, a beagle, and Teddy, a boxer/shepherd mix. One Saturday, we watched J'aime while Karen took Teddy to the annual Mutt Strut held by the local humane society. J'aime liked cats, but Clio spent the entire afternoon hissing and growling at him, despite the fact that he was at least three times her size. After three or four hours of taunting J'aime, Clio finally decided to take a nap in her bed by the kitchen door. J'aime thought Clio was in the living room with us, so to avoid her, he took the long route all the way around the living and dining rooms to the kitchen to get some food. He had no idea she was in the bed by the kitchen door. Clio woke up just as J'aime walked by the bed and was about to go into the kitchen. At that point, Clio hissed. Never before had I seen a dog jump so high. Once his feet hit the floor, J'aime ran back to the bedroom, tail between his legs, and stayed there until my sister-in-law picked him up.

A few months after Clio had her hind leg amputated, Karen stopped by our house with Teddy. Teddy hadn't yet met Clio, and since we didn't know whether he would like cats, we played it safe and shut the kitchen door. Because it is a swinging door, we placed a large magazine rack on the other side to prevent Teddy from pushing it open. Clio didn't like a closed door, and in her mind, there was no dog too big or too mean whom she couldn't take on. So, she lay down on the other side of the door.

Seeing her three paws sticking out from under the door and deciding that she could not afford to lose another limb, I screamed, "Oh no! Clio get away from the . . ." But before I could run to push her paws back under the door, Teddy went racing for the door and with brute force pushed it open. That day, Clio may have set a record for the fifty-yard dash. She ran to the master bedroom and dove under the bed, which is so low to the ground that she could barely fit under it. She positioned herself in the middle so Teddy couldn't reach her. We had to pry Teddy away from the bed and then close the bedroom door so Clio wouldn't try again to antagonize an eighty-pound dog. I think even Clio recognized that her bravery may have morphed into stupidity that day, but it still didn't prevent her from being fearless.

When Clio was six years old, I rescued a dog, a Shar Pei, who had been abandoned in our neighborhood. His owners, who didn't want him back, called him Hatchmo. I had great difficulty catching Hatchmo because every time I approached him, he would growl. Eventually I was able to pet him, but when he growled I would pull back in fear, not knowing whether he would attack me.

I found a Shar Pei rescue group several hours away that would accept him and help find his "forever home." The problem was that I could not take Hatchmo to the rescue group until the weekend, and we needed to keep him confined for the next few days since our yard was not fenced and he would not allow us to place a leash on him. I decided to keep him in our garage until the weekend.

Although Hatchmo was fearful of most humans, he seemed to be interested in my cats. While I was cooking dinner, I would leave the inside door open between the kitchen and the garage so Hatchmo could peer into the kitchen through the glass door. Dickens would watch Hatchmo and seemed interested in getting to know him. Clio, however, would walk up to the door, hiss, and growl. Eventually, Hatchmo would begin barking and growling, and we would have to close the door to the garage to prevent a disaster.

Hatchmo eventually found a home, and fortunately Clio's behavior didn't turn him against cats. He was adopted by a family with another Shar Pei and a cat, probably one more like Dickens than Clio.

All these antics and near misses with dogs didn't prevent Clio from taking on other animals, including wild ones. One night we heard the most horrible commotion coming from the den. Jeff and I jumped out of bed and went into the den, where we found Clio on the sill of the picture window, hissing at a large raccoon who was positioned on the outside window ledge. The raccoon was hurling himself against the window and baring his teeth. The glass in that window was not security glass and could easily be broken if a twenty-five-pound raccoon continued to pound against it. I decided that before we ended up with a broken picture window and a raccoon in our den, we would get Clio out of the room and close the door. Clio fought like crazy when I removed her from the window. Apparently she thought this raccoon was no match for an eleven-pound, one-eyed, three-legged cat with cattitude.

According to English zoologist and writer Desmond Morris: "Alexander the Great, Napoleon, and Hitler . . . were apparently terrified of small felines. If you want to conquer the world, you had better not share even a moment with an animal that refuses to be conquered at any price, by anyone." I like to imagine Clio opining that if cats could strike fear in the likes of conquerors and dictators such as these, then large dogs, raccoons, and other wild animals were no problem for her. It was evident that Clio viewed herself as a fierce lioness rather than a three-legged, one-eyed house cat. What a lesson for me! Clio was a great teacher and an effective therapist. I, too, began facing difficult issues head on and began seeing myself as a smart, attractive, successful person and not the ugly, fat, stupid person I used to see in the mirror.

# 14

## Clio, the Therapy Cat

*There are two means of refuge from the miseries of
life—music and cats.* —ALBERT SCHWEITZER

THE YEAR CLIO TURNED FIFTEEN WAS ANOTHER ONE OF THOSE
years I wanted to forget. After seven years of living with us, my mother,
whose health had continued to deteriorate, became less able to care
for herself. Every weekday morning, I would awaken at four to take
care of her before I went to work. I had to change her sheets when
she'd had an accident in the middle of the night, bathe her, dress her,
help her to the bathroom, and then prepare her lunch. Midyear her
condition worsened as she lost almost all her mobility. She eventually became extremely ill and had to be placed in a long-term care facility. We had hoped she would recover her strength and walk again,
but that never occurred. Moreover, her dementia was getting worse,
and she in no way could be left alone for any amount of time. The one
bright spot in this whole ordeal was that she remembered my husband, the cats, and me.

Having come to the decision that my mother needed twenty-four-
hour care, I began the difficult and trying task of finding a nursing
home that would accept Medicaid once her savings were depleted. My
mother had been in a private-pay nursing home for six months and
had connected with many of the staff, but there was no way I could

afford the $6,000 a month to keep her there. Finding a *good* nursing home that accepted Medicaid was not easy. It goes back to the adage "You get what you pay for." When you aren't paying the bills and Medicaid is (and paying the long-term care facility much less), the care at most is less than satisfactory. Fortunately, I was able to find a decent nursing home. However, the transition seemed traumatic for my mother. I was constantly getting calls from her complaining they had not fed her (they had, but she had forgotten).

"They didn't feed me again," she would say.

"Mom, I'm sure they did."

"Well, if they did, why don't I remember?"

"Are you hungry?"

"No."

"Well, then, they probably fed you. Maybe the food wasn't that memorable."

"I'd remember if it weren't memorable."

"Okay, I'll call them and see what's going on."

I would hang up the phone, call the nursing home, and talk to her nurse, who would say my mother had been fed and had eaten everything. The nurse would even tell me what she had to eat. Then ten minutes later, my phone would ring.

"Hi. You know they didn't feed me again."

"Mom, you called me ten minutes ago. I called them, and they said you had Swiss steak, mashed potatoes, and green beans for lunch. They said you ate it all."

"Well, they are lying. Besides, I would remember if I had that to eat. I love Swiss steak."

"Mom, I think you've forgotten they fed you and forgotten you called me."

"I would remember if I had called you . . . and I would have remembered if I'd eaten."

And so the conversation would go.

My mother eventually adjusted to her new home, but it was difficult for the both of us. The change was particularly hard on Clio, who lost not only one of her favorite human companions, but her endless stream of snacks and tuna treats.

Then, just when I thought things were going well, my mother suffered a stroke. The stroke affected her right side and her ability to swallow. Prior to this, she had become wheelchair bound but at least had the strength to use the bathroom and eat with her right hand. After the stroke, however, she had to wear a diaper and be changed in bed. She had no strength on her right side and could not balance herself on the toilet. What is worse, she lost her ability to swallow (and my mother loved to eat) and had to be fed through a tube in her stomach.

Visiting her was difficult because she would ask for food, and I would have to explain time and time again that she'd had a stroke and wasn't able to swallow. She didn't understand this because she felt like she could swallow. What she couldn't comprehend was that if she swallowed, she would aspirate the food, and it would go into her lungs. If that happened, she would develop pneumonia. Moreover, because of the dementia, she could not remember why the tube was in her stomach and kept trying to pull it out. My evenings and weekends were spent at the nursing home, attempting to calm her down and make her understand why she couldn't eat and needed a feeding tube. Luckily, the speech therapist there was able to work with her, and eventually her swallow function came back. Then the problem was that the food had to be ground up and sometimes pureed, and nothing is more unappetizing than pureed food.

While facing all these challenges with my mother, I was also having a hard time at work. The Great Recession had hit the nation. Several years earlier, I had taken a new job managing a trade association representing one type of real estate investment, and that industry was adversely affected when the economy took a nosedive. So not only was I caring for my mother on evenings and weekends, but I was also trying desperately to salvage the organization despite declining revenues. Members who knew no financial hardship would complain that they couldn't go to Starbucks every day to get their white chocolate mocha lattes.

In spite of the ordeal with my mother, I never missed more than one or two days of work that year. However, between the demands of work and my mother, I had no time to myself. I knew that I couldn't afford to take any time off because my board president had no empathy whatsoever about my plight. He was more concerned with his own personal financial woes since his income had been cut from several million dollars to just a few million. In fact, on the day my mother suffered a stroke and I was with her in the emergency ward, he emailed me asking for a document. I emailed him back on my phone that I couldn't get it for him right then because my mother had just had a stroke. His answer was, "I don't care. I need that document now." It was nothing urgent and nothing he couldn't have found on our website or called someone else in the office to retrieve, but obviously he couldn't be inconvenienced.

Not only was I dealing with a narcissistic board president, but the other board members had taken on the unethical attitude that the association existed specifically for them, and our conference was a location for setting up meetings with their clients and using association money to pay their clients' hotel and travel expenditures. In some cases their behavior was not only unethical but illegal. For example, immediately after I left the association the following year, the new board president was arrested and eventually went to jail for operating a Ponzi scheme and defrauding several investors who had trusted their life savings with her. She had used her affiliation and position of power with the association to start her dubious and illegal new business. And I can't even say how many others were facing charges from the Securities and Exchange Commission or being sued by investors. Work was not a fun place to be, and my ethical values were being seriously tested. What's worse, amid all the problems with my mother and my job, Dickens died suddenly.

Except for putting on a few extra pounds after his thirteenth birthday, Dickens was basically a healthy cat. His only two ailments during his life were a cyst on his back and an abscessed tooth. The fact that he had very few health problems was good because he couldn't handle the slightest pain. After I brought Dickens home from having the cyst removed, he ran into the garage and hid under the car. When I managed to extract him (and the bright orange bandage he had removed) from under the car and brought him inside, he began running around like he was crazy. I assume he was trying to run away from the pain. What's worse, he wouldn't let me give him any of his pain medication. According to a biblical verse from Corinthians, "God only gives you what you can handle." But Dickens couldn't handle the removal of even a small cyst.

Since Dickens always received a good health report from the vet, it was a complete shock when only a few days after his birthday in July, he suddenly became ill and died. The year before he died, Dickens violated Clio's rule of never sitting on my lap. Either he knew that she was getting older and was not as strong, or he knew that his time on this earth was short and he wanted to be with me as much as he could. He started sitting on my lap instead of next to me while I ate breakfast, which usually meant I had to spend quite some time getting the black cat hair off my clothes before I went to work. He greeted me in the evening, and then after dinner when I would sit down in the den, or even lie in bed watching television, he would jump on my lap or stomach and spend the rest of the evening with me. Even when I turned on my side in bed to go to sleep, he would be on top of me, eventually retreating to the end of the bed where Clio was sleeping. It was as if he didn't care whether Clio hit him for sitting on me. He was finally standing up for his rights.

One Friday in July, I attended the funeral of a friend's mother who had died suddenly of a heart attack. After leaving the funeral, I was extremely upset over my friend's loss and debated whether to return to work or instead go home. Since there were only two hours left in the workday, I decided to go home. The minute I came in the door and sat down in the living room, Dickens joined me on my lap and we spent over two hours together. I played string with him and then fixed dinner. After dinner, he went off by himself, which was not unusual since he had spent time with me that afternoon.

That night, he didn't join us in bed. The next morning, I got up early to go to the grocery store. When I returned, Dickens jumped up on the kitchen table to investigate the various grocery bags. As I was unloading the last bag, he jumped off the table, and I noticed he had a slight limp. I told my husband, and we both agreed that he and Clio had probably gotten into a fight and she'd bitten him. I then went about doing my other errands and visiting my mother at the nursing home.

That afternoon, I joined Dickens on the floor in the living room and tried playing string with him. He played some and then got up and staggered away. Now, I was more worried but decided that he was still okay. However, he didn't eat dinner that evening and hid behind the couch in the den. As his condition worsened, my husband and I both decided that we would see how he was in the morning and, if necessary, take him to the emergency clinic.

When I awakened on Sunday morning, Dickens was not waiting for me to feed him. In fact, he was still behind the couch in the den. I moved the couch to pick him up, and we spent an hour together with him on my lap. When he got off my lap, he staggered like a drunken sailor to the litter box and tried to go, and when he couldn't, he sat down in the litter box and didn't seem to have the energy to get out.

When I told my husband that something was wrong with Dickens, Jeff said, "You'd better call the emergency clinic. I'll get dressed, and we can take him there."

When I called the vet clinic, they said there was a four-hour wait, so we decided to stay at home with Dickens and then take him later that afternoon. In the afternoon, we put Dickens into the pet carrier (and for a sick cat, he sure made a lot of noise and put up quite a struggle) and drove off to the emergency clinic. Fortunately, the vet was able to see him right away. At first the vet thought he had diabetes, but a blood test revealed that his kidneys weren't functioning. They wanted to keep him overnight, hydrate him, and do more tests. When we left the clinic, we were hopeful that Dickens would be home in a few days.

Early the next day, before I went in to work, I drove to the emergency clinic to see Dickens. When they took him out of the cage and put him in my lap, he started purring loudly. Then the vet came in to talk with me. His test results weren't good. Dickens had only one kidney. They discovered that one had shriveled up and died, and the other one was not functioning. They said they would see what they could do, but he wasn't urinating, and the poisons in his system were building up and causing congestive heart failure.

By that evening when I went to see him, his beautiful black shiny coat had turned a dirty, dull brown. He didn't even purr when they put him in my lap. Despite all they were trying, nothing seemed to be working, and he was getting worse.

The next day in a panic, I called Dr. Dave for advice, and he called the emergency clinic to get a copy of Dickens's reports and ultrasound. Dr. Dave thought that the ultrasound showed an infarction on the renal vein. In layman's terms, a blood clot had been thrown off, and it shut down his one functioning kidney.

In response to this information, I asked Dr. Dave, "Isn't there anything we can do? Dialysis? A kidney transplant?"

"No, Kathy," he said. "We don't have anywhere in this state for dialysis. The closest facility for transplants is over four hundred miles away, but let me check into it."

When Dr. Dave called me back, he said there was a huge waiting list for kidney transplants and all the treatments were experimental with little chance of success. My heart sank.

Later in the morning, I received another call from the emergency clinic. There truly was no hope for Dickens. I asked if they could drain the fluids so I could explore some options. They said yes, but they would have to sedate him to do that, and they doubted if he would survive the sedation. Upset and distraught, I called my husband. I could barely speak because I was crying so hard.

"Jeff . . . Dickens's kidneys aren't working . . . I don't want to put him down," I said.

Jeff responded, "But Kathy, he's miserable. You know how Dickens hates pain. I think it's the most humane thing to do."

"I guess. Can you come home and go with me to the clinic?"

"I'll be right there."

Although I didn't want to part with Dickens, I had to make a choice. Most likely, he would not live another day, and he was in misery. Therefore, we made the decision to have Dickens euthanized. As sad as I was to lose Dickens and as much as I hated to witness this, I decided to be with him when he took his last breath. I had remembered one of the Top Ten Commandments for a Responsible Pet Owner, which says: "Go with me on the difficult journeys. *Never* say, 'I can't bear to watch it,' or, 'Let it happen in my absence.' Everything is easier for me if you are there. Above all, remember that I love you."

When we arrived at the clinic, we spent several minutes with Dickens, who looked into my eyes. I knew he was miserable, but he knew that I loved him. We allowed the vet to come back in and administer the first dose of anesthesia and then the second, lethal dose. Dickens opened his mouth and breathed for the last time.

We had Dickens cremated and the box containing his remains inscribed with "Dickens—Our big guy and friend forever." Every Christmas, we place his ashes under the tree in the living room since he so loved sleeping there during the holiday season.

🐾

The passing of Dickens, my almost unbearable work situation, and my mother's worsening health meant that if anyone needed rescuing at that time, it was my husband and me. Amid all these travails, Clio now took on the role of therapy cat. That wasn't particularly surprising given that she had been a therapy cat to us previously. Clio had done so much for me by restoring my self-esteem, building my self-confidence, improving my relationship with my mother, and bringing laughter back into my life. She was the one bright spot for my husband, my mother, and me. A few years earlier, when my mother suffered a serious fall in her own home and was about to undergo a very risky surgery (with a 30 to 40 percent chance of making it through surgery), I brought her a photo of Clio and told her that she needed to make it through the surgery for her. My mother beat the odds and later told me that she wanted to live because she knew Clio and I needed her. And then there were the many times when I was sad and lonely (before I met my current husband), and Clio would jump on my chest while I was crying and try her best to comfort me.

❧

Since I was away from home a lot, either traveling for work or visiting my mother in the nursing home, Jeff spent a lot of time alone. He never really complained, but I know it must have been difficult. However, Clio was there to comfort him. She would sit on his lap while they watched television and purr loudly to express her contentment. This proved to be very soothing to Jeff, and he grew close to her. She was also there for me when I returned from my travels and would sit on my lap (for the few minutes I sat down) and sleep with me at night. Of course her antics kept us laughing, which was great comic relief for both of us. And even though she had had a complicated relationship with Dickens, when we returned that day from the vet clinic without him, I think Clio knew he was gone. She came up to us as we sat on the couch crying, jumped up on our laps straddling us both, and lay down quietly as we cried. Together, we all three mourned the loss of Dickens and comforted one another.

Before Dickens passed, Clio was not an official therapy cat, but that changed when I decided that my mother needed Clio to cheer her up. My mother loved Clio and would always ask about her. When we had lunch, the first question she would ask was, "So, how is Clio?" Then every other question would be about Clio: "Did you feed her before you came here?" followed by "Make sure you give her some tuna treats and a hug from me."

When she spoke Clio's name or saw her picture, my mother would beam. I had never seen such a huge smile on her face. That's when I decided that even though Clio hated traveling in the car, I would take her to see my mother since it was difficult to bring my mother home. Every other Saturday I would place Clio in the pet carrier and together we would visit my mother and other residents at the nursing home.

The first time we went, she meowed all the way. However, the second time we went, she meowed until we got to the end of our street, where it dead-ended, and you had to turn either left or right. On that trip she figured out that turning left meant going to Dr. Dave's, and the meowing needed to continue and intensify into bloodcurdling screams, but turning right meant she would be the center of attention among the nursing home residents. Being in the limelight suited Clio well. Therefore, the remainder of the ride was quiet, and all I could hear was an occasional purr.

My mother was ecstatic when I brought Clio to see her. Residents would pass by my mother's room and see Clio, then roll their wheelchairs or walk in and fawn over her, petting her and telling us how beautiful she was. Clio loved the attention, so every time I brought her to the nursing home, I would make several stops before visiting my mother. Once I arrived at my mother's room, I would take Clio out of the carrier. My mother didn't have the strength to hold Clio anymore, so I would hold her while my mother petted and conversed with her. Then, after about thirty minutes, I would take Clio to the rest of her adoring fans who weren't able to come to my mother's room to see her. The whole time, she ate up the attention.

The nursing home residents were amazed by the fact that Clio got around so well with three legs and one eye. I always thought that she provided them with a great deal of inspiration. In fact, when I showed up without her and ran into her fans, they would always ask about her and want to know when she was coming back to visit. One of the residents would say, "We all love *our* little Clio."

Even the nurses and aides would comment on how therapeutic and inspirational Clio was to the residents. She had become a true therapy cat. Not only had she helped my husband and me during that difficult year, but she was a bright spot in my mother's life, as well as in the lives of many of the nursing home's other residents. Clio's true calling, saving others (which we knew all along), was formally recognized.

# Goodbye, My Sweet Friend

TRIBUTE TO A BEST FRIEND

*Sunlight streams through the window pane, unto a spot on the floor....*
*then I remember, it's where you used to lie but now you are no more.*

*Our feet walk down a hall of carpet, and muted echoes sound....*
*then I remember, it's where your paws would joyously abound.*

*A voice is heard along the road, and up beyond the hill....*
*then I remember, it can't be yours ... your golden voice is still.*

*But I'll take that vacant spot of floor, and empty muted hall....*
*lay them with the absent voice, and unused dish, along the wall.*

*I'll wrap these treasured memories in a blanket of my love....*
*and keep them for my loving friend, until we meet above.*

—AUTHOR UNKNOWN (FROM DR. DAVE)

CLIO WAS ALWAYS A FIGHTER. SHE HAD SURVIVED TWO BOUTS with cancer and four surgeries despite her heart murmur, eating a poisonous plant, and numerous close calls around the house. It was almost inconceivable that she would not beat the odds when faced with future ailments.

Almost one year after losing Dickens, we noticed that Clio was having difficulty sitting down. She would go round and round before sitting down, then sit down very, very slowly. We thought it was her arthritis acting up again but decided to take her to Dr. Dave, although she had just seen him a few months earlier. We had been hydrating her three times a week for several months to improve her kidney function because a blood test revealed elevated BUN and creatinine levels. The treatments seemed to be working, and her last lab results (only a month previously) indicated that her kidney function was normal. When Dr. Dave examined her, he told us he didn't think arthritis was the only problem. He did another blood test, and to our surprise, her BUN and creatinine levels were extremely high. It was Thursday, and he asked us to hydrate her twice a day for the rest of the weekend and bring her back on Monday to see if her kidney function had improved.

We took Clio home and followed Dr. Dave's instructions. Hydrating Clio was quite the challenge. She seemed to have a sixth sense about when it was time to hydrate, and she would try to hide. Immobilizing a meowing—or, more precisely, howling and struggling—cat while trying to stab her with a needle and hold the hydration bag high enough so the fluid flows through the tube for about ten minutes was difficult, to say the least. Once during this process, Clio struggled so hard that I ended up with the hydration needle in my own arm.

We had hoped that the hydration would work, but as the weekend wore on, Clio's energy level declined precipitously. She spent most of the weekend sleeping and had great difficulty walking. Before now, missing a hind leg had not slowed her down, but this illness changed that.

With heavy hearts, we took Clio to see Dr. Dave on Monday and anxiously awaited the results of the blood tests. Her creatinine and

BUN levels were higher than ever, and Dr. Dave said they could try hospitalizing her so that they could hydrate her continuously, noting that this might help jump-start her kidneys. We decided to leave her with him and see if this treatment worked.

Of course she fought them tooth and nail when they put in the intravenous tube the next day. In fact, Dr. Dave had to call me to see if I approved them sedating her to get the tube in since she had managed to rip out the first one. We knew it was dangerous to put a cat in this condition under anesthesia. I was at a conference about sixty miles away and kept calling the clinic to check on her. Luckily, she made it through the procedure, and I was hopeful that our little fighter would beat this illness and live several more years.

During that difficult week, we visited Clio daily. I would cook chicken, grind it up, and make chicken broth. Her appetite came back, and she would clean her plate every night. By the end of the week, Dr. Dave did more blood tests, and her kidney function was back to normal. Although he mentioned that this might not last, we were delighted at her progress and took her home. We had made up several special beds for her with plenty of blankets because she always seemed cold. However, once we brought her home, she didn't seem as active, and her appetite diminished once again.

We were very depressed and questioned whether we should go to the state fair that Friday as we had planned. But the more we thought about it, we decided it was better for us to get our minds off Clio and allow her to rest. While we were home with her, she didn't want to sleep. So we went, and much to our surprise, when we came home that evening, Clio was up and about. When we walked into the living room, she lay down by a basket and, in her usual "look at me, aren't I cute" mode, slid toward the basket and started clawing it, and then of course looked back to make sure we were watching.

During the next few days Clio even played, and in the evenings she would spend time on our laps sleeping. However, she also exhibited some troubling behaviors. She seemed to have difficulty drinking and had little appetite. Moreover, she would try to climb to the top of the back of the couch. She was seeking high ground—often a sign in animals that they are sick and want to get to safety before being killed or eaten by another animal.

Yet, overall, Clio seemed to be on the mend. Although she wasn't completely back to her usual self, she seemed to be making progress. Two weeks passed, and we took her to the vet for follow-up bloodwork. Then we received the bad news. Dr. Dave informed us that her behavior didn't match her kidney function numbers. Once again, the numbers were slowly rising. We went back to hydrating her daily to see if that would help and had weekly laser treatment appointments at the vet to help her arthritis.

There would be times when we were encouraged. Then there were other times that saddened our hearts beyond belief.

One night after dinner out, I brought home a doggie bag with a piece of chicken in it. Clio immediately smelled the chicken and started following me around, meowing loudly. I put the chicken in the blender and chopped it up for her. She practically tore the plate out of my hand to get to the chicken. Then a week or so later, we again came home from dinner with a piece of chicken, but we couldn't find Clio. After a search, we discovered her in a corner of the bathroom. She couldn't figure out how to get out, and she started meowing pitifully. Dr. Dave had told us that kidney failure can lead to dementia, and it was clear that dementia had set in and was getting worse. That night, we put her on the couch with us, and she insisted that she needed to be on top of it and even tried to climb the bookcase. She was too weak to do either, so we put her up on the back of the couch, but she just kept meowing.

One Saturday late in September, I took Clio to the vet for a laser treatment. She was still receiving treatments to help with her arthritis. Although getting her to the vet was a challenge, once there, she loved the treatments and would purr loudly. She did the same that Saturday, but she was still weak. Knowing that she might not last much longer, I decided to stop off and see my mother at the nursing home. I thought she would love to see Clio one last time.

When I arrived, my mother was not doing very well, but she did acknowledge Clio's presence. She so loved seeing Clio, and even when she wasn't feeling good, she loved to be around her. Unfortunately, I had to spend the next twenty minutes trying to locate a nurse. While I was gone, I left Clio in her carrier in my mother's room. Once I finally convinced the nursing home staff that they needed to call a doctor for my mother and was assured they would do so, Clio and I said our goodbyes and left for home.

When we got there, I let Clio out of the carrier and she immediately urinated on the floor. I thought that perhaps she had not gone to the litter box before we went to the vet and to visit my mother and simply could not wait any longer. Unfortunately, that was the beginning of Clio's incontinence. Later that afternoon she lay down on my lap, and about a half hour later when she was sound asleep, I felt something warm and wet on my leg. She had urinated all over me and didn't even know it.

That night, Clio's dementia got worse, and she wandered around the house meowing. I put her in the spare bed and covered it with piddle pads, which she wet several times during the night. The next week, her loss of bladder control worsened, and it became harder for her to drink. I spent the next several nights with her. Finally, I called Dr. Dave and asked, "Is it time?"

"Yes, Kathy, it's time," he answered. "This is best for her."

I then said, "Dr. Dave, you know how much Clio hates to go to your office. I can't bear the thought of having her spend her last hour in a carrier and her last minutes in your office."

"I'll come to your house," he replied. "Is eleven o'clock tomorrow morning ok?"

"Yes, thank you."

I was glad he would come to our house, but I dreaded the next few hours knowing that I had signed Clio's death warrant.

With the image of Dickens dying in my arms still fresh in my memory, I had hoped against hope that Clio would just pass in her sleep. However, it looked like that was not going to happen. The night before Dr. Dave's house call was awful. I decided to spend the entire night with her on the bed, which I had covered in piddle pads. Clio fell asleep purring on a pillow.

The next morning the sun was out, and it was a beautiful fall day. Clio ate a little but didn't leave the bed. She was looking out the window listening to the birds chirp when Dr. Dave arrived a few minutes before eleven. Normally, Clio would run when she smelled anyone from the vet clinic. (In fact, she even ran when we received an appointment reminder postcard from the vet—that is how keen her sense of smell was.) She didn't move, but as Dr. Dave was administering the drug, the phone rang. The call was from a solicitor, and for once, a solicitor's call was appreciated since Clio was momentarily distracted by the ringing telephone. She then quietly passed away.

My husband and I spent the remainder of the afternoon on the couch holding each other and sobbing. Clio, the spunky little runt of the litter who'd kept us on our toes and was indeed quite the survivor, was gone. No more sweet purring cat to comfort us. No more silly antics to make us laugh. No more little survivor to give us hope.

As with Dickens, we had Clio cremated and put her remains in a box with her photo. We placed her next to Dickens. Engraved on the box was "Clio—Our beautiful and spunky little girl." Every time we passed the hearth or looked at the box, we were reminded just how heartbroken we were. The holes in our hearts seemed too massive for repair. First, we'd lost Dickens, and now Clio. We definitely needed a miracle to save us this time.

That miracle came in the form of two rescue cats: Jackson, a little stray cat who lived in a field near a friend's house, and Benny, a shelter cat who was soon to be deemed unadoptable.

While I was talking with a friend, she told me that a little gray cat had shown up in her field and asked me if I was interested. I said it was too soon to think about another cat, but I knew that part of me really wanted and needed a cat. She asked me several times, and finally I said I'd try to convince my husband to go look at the cat.

After several days of pleading, I convinced Jeff to go with me to look at him. However, Jeff made it clear that absolutely under no circumstances were we getting another cat so soon after Clio's death. On a Tuesday evening, we went to look at the cat. All the way there my husband repeatedly told me, "No cat. I just can't take the heartbreak again."

"Yes, I know," I said. "I just agreed that I would at least look at him."

When we arrived at my friend's drive, she called for the cat. He soon popped his head up like a meerkat and then came running to my friend. She picked him up and handed this cute little ball of gray fur to Jeff. Right away he put his paw on Jeff's cheek and started purring. Within nanoseconds, and without asking me, Jeff said, "We'll take him." I was shocked, especially after he had insisted that we would not take another cat so soon after Clio's passing. We packed up the gray cat (soon to be named Jackson) and headed home. None of us—Jeff, Jackson, nor I—could have been happier.

Jackson took to his new surroundings right away and became my husband's new best friend. We immediately made an appointment with Dr. Dave. We certainly didn't want to take in a cat only to find out he belonged to someone else, or he was gravely ill. Jackson purred all the way to the vet clinic, but when Dr. Dave tried to draw blood, Jackson went ballistic. Vicky, the same vet tech who had been with the clinic during all our trials and tribulations with Clio, looked like she had been through a war after trying to hold Jackson down. He finally had to be sedated. Fortunately, the news was good. Jackson was in excellent shape, and he had no chip so he didn't belong to anyone but us.

We were scheduled to go out of town for the weekend, and we recruited Jeff's sister to look in on our new friend. Before we left to go on our "mini vacation," however, we went to PetSmart to get an identification tag for Jackson. While there we walked by the adoption cages because I told Jeff that maybe we should get a companion for Jackson before he became too territorial. Sure enough, my husband found another cat. His name was Benny, and the information on him indicated he was a "very sweet cat who loved other animals." Poor Benny had been in PetSmart from animal control for three months, and it looked like he was headed back to the shelter. Benny was not as adoptable as the others there because he wasn't a lap cat, and he was older—about three years old. Jeff was attracted to him because Benny, who was cramped in a small cage, was occupying his time trying to catch a small gnat. Jeff felt that behavior was a sign of intelligence. We both agreed that given Benny's sweet nature and his love of other animals, he would be the perfect companion for Jackson.

We didn't adopt him that night because we were going out of town and didn't want to introduce another cat into the household and then leave. So we thought that after we returned from vacation, we would go back to PetSmart and check out the pets. If Benny was still there, we'd adopt him. Otherwise, we'd take another cat.

When we got home, we couldn't stop thinking about Benny. We had fallen in love with him and didn't want to chance losing him, but we still felt it wouldn't be a good idea to bring him into our home and then leave. I immediately called PetSmart. They said they couldn't hold him but would call if someone else came in to adopt him. The entire weekend we worried that Benny would be adopted by someone else. We also worried about our newest friend, Jackson, who was "home alone." We called Jeff's sister every night to make sure he was okay.

Fortunately, no one else adopted Benny, and when we returned from our weekend getaway, we went to PetSmart immediately to adopt him even though we were both dead tired. We decided to have the onsite vet check him out. Aside from being overweight, he was in good shape. So we drove home several hours later with Benny in a cardboard box. Benny hated being in the box, and he clawed through it and dug into my husband's leg. But Jeff didn't seem to care. He had found another new friend.

When we arrived home, we thought Jackson would immediately take to Benny because he had spent several days alone and certainly would appreciate a companion. Unfortunately, that wasn't the case, and Jackson threw a fit. Jackson had only been in our home for four days, but he had decided that this was his house and no one else's. However, Benny didn't care. He ignored Jackson's hissy fits and was simply happy to be out of a cage.

We separated the two of them and put Benny in the spare bedroom with a few toys, food, and a litter box. Jackson spent most of the night outside the bedroom door hissing, but Benny was having a blast inside. He played with all his toys for most of the night. We could hear him tossing his toys in the air and then chasing after them. He was the ultimate party animal, and he didn't need anyone else to party with. Benny's antics helped alleviate the deep sorrow we were feeling after the loss of Clio. We just hoped that Benny and Jackson would work out their differences so we could become a happy family again.

Over the next few days, Jackson vacillated between throwing "hissy fits," growling outside the bedroom door, and becoming withdrawn. Jackson would hide under the bed and not let my husband hold or pet him. Finally, after a week, we decided to let Benny out of the bedroom so the two of them could settle their differences. At first, it didn't look like our strategy would work. However, Benny's easygoing nature eased the situation. When Jackson went up to Benny and hissed, Benny would stop for a minute, look at him, then walk away. Benny was so self-confident and so happy to have a home; he was not going to let this little upstart ruin his fun. He would have liked a friend, but if Jackson didn't want to be his friend, that was fine too. He finally had a home, and he was grateful for that.

Benny's nonchalant attitude worked. Jackson didn't like being ignored, and soon he went up to Benny, stopped hissing, and started licking him. Not only did they make up with each other, but they ended up being inseparable "best buddies."

Benny and Jackson turned out to be the miracle we needed to help us after the loss of Clio. But the biggest miracle of all occurred when the spirits of Clio and Dickens came back to keep us company. They finally convinced me that there indeed was life after death and that a higher being was watching over me and had sent Clio and all the other wonderful cats in my life to me in my times of greatest need. The restoration of my spiritual beliefs was particularly important because three months after losing Clio, my mother died.

My mother and I had grown remarkably close after the passing of my father, and our bond grew even stronger after my divorce. We had gone through so much together. She was my inspiration. I could not imagine a life without her and so regretted the fifteen years during my first marriage in which we grew apart. Not only did Clio and Dickens help bring us back together during the last years of her life, but now in their passing, they gave me the greatest gift of all—the belief in an afterlife. As I sat by my mother's bedside in hospice during the last few days of her life, I knew I could finally let go and say goodbye because I would see her again, as well as my father, other family members, and my pets.

# 16

# Hello Again

*I believe cats to be spirits come to earth. A cat, I am sure,*
*could walk on a cloud without coming through.*

—JULES VERNE

AFTER I LOST MY FATHER, I ALWAYS HOPED THAT I WOULD SEE
him again in Heaven, but as I learned increasingly about life and religion, my faith in an afterlife and a benevolent God faded. Some
of my relatives and friends were religious, and they continuously reminded me that because my mother and I didn't go to church regularly,
we would not be among those chosen to enter the gates of Heaven.
Moreover, when I asked whether my former pets would be with me
in Heaven, they told me, "No. Animals don't have souls."

I wanted to believe, and I wanted to be with my father again one day,
as well as my mother, but I couldn't fathom that a loving God would
not allow my pets to be with me. I shared the same sentiments of this
anonymous author of a pet epitaph: "No heaven will not ever Heaven
be unless my cats are there to welcome me."

Increasingly, I concluded that some so-called "Christians" were
hypocrites. What they did in life and their judgmental nature bore
no resemblance to the teachings of Christianity. So I constantly wondered whether God was as harsh as they made him out to be, and
I pretty much decided that if no animals were allowed in Heaven

(apparently because they had no souls), then maybe Heaven wasn't the place for me, if indeed it did exist.

Many times in my life I felt my prayers were answered and that cats had come to my rescue, but never had I had an experience that made me genuinely believe that there was an afterlife. However, Clio and Dickens made me believe again.

The first experience came two to three days after Dickens died, while I was staring at my computer screen at work with tears streaming down my face. I just couldn't believe that Dickens was gone. Then I noticed some glowing particles in the air around my computer. It looked like what we see when dust particles are caught in glowing sunlight. Sunshine was indeed streaming through my window, but the particles weren't in the sunbeam. They were in front of my computer screen in the form of a big round ball about the size of Dickens. As I watched the glowing ball of particles, I began to smile as I thought about how beautiful Dickens's yellow eyes were. Then it occurred to me that maybe he was sending me a message, letting me know he was okay and no longer in pain.

In spite of this experience, the shock of Dickens's sudden death was still with me. A few days later at work, I was sitting at a table in my office and again began to cry. Then I looked out the window and saw a beautiful black-and-yellow butterfly. The butterfly reminded me of Dickens and his beautiful black fur and yellow eyes. My office was on the second floor, with no trees or bushes around the windows. I stared at the butterfly and began to smile. Again, I think Dickens was sending me a message.

I'd never fully believed that there was an afterlife, but now my skepticism was beginning to wane. And these were not the only afterlife experiences either I or my husband would have with Dickens.

One day when Jeff's sister came to visit while I was traveling, they were sitting in our living room talking when they heard a cat jump off the table. The problem was that Clio was curled up next to Jeff, and there was no other cat in the house. And on a couple of occasions my husband told me he saw the shadow of a big cat in the hallway. Again, it wasn't Clio because she was with him.

I once felt a cat brush against me, and when I looked up, I saw Clio asleep on the bed. Then one night in bed I felt something heavy on my feet and thought it was Clio. I sat up to push her off my feet because they were falling asleep, then realized she was asleep on the other side of the bed. And sometimes I would hear water dripping in the bathtub (a favorite watering hole of Dickens) during the night, but when I got up there would be no water dripping.

However, the most convincing sign of an afterlife occurred the night before we were to have Clio euthanized. I spent the night with Clio, who was lying on a pillow. Given her delicate state, I wanted to be close to her so she wouldn't fall off the bed and spend her last hours in pain. In the middle of the night, I was awakened by what I thought was a cat walking next to me. I quickly sat up to stop Clio from falling off the bed, but when I turned on the light, I saw that she was sound asleep and snoring on the pillow next to mine, where I'd put her. I am convinced now that Dickens came back to tell Clio it would be all right (and maybe to let her know that she, too, could come back for a visit).

Unfortunately, right after Clio died I didn't have any afterlife experiences with her, which made me think she would not come back to visit us. Then a few months after we got Jackson, I noticed him acting strangely. Now, I know that cats act strangely and often chase things that aren't there, but one thing he did was particularly peculiar and reminiscent of Clio. Clio would regularly run up to Dickens and bite his butt. And now, Jackson would suddenly turn around and bat at something near his backside, then take off running as if to get away from something or someone. Occasionally, as he was running away, he would appear to be knocked down, but no one was there to knock him down. He also started taking on some of Clio's behaviors, like lying on the floor near this one basket, scratching it, and then looking back to see if anyone was watching. We were beginning to suspect he had a mentor, and it wasn't Benny or us.

My husband, who has more of a sixth sense than I do, experienced Clio's presence several times. More than once he noticed a gray-and-white cat curled up in the chair in our bedroom. At first he thought it was Benny, but then Benny would come walking in from the hall and the apparition would disappear. He also saw a gray-and-white cat in the hallway several times.

I was a little skeptical since I had never had a supernatural experience with Clio. Then one night, Benny was intensely playing with his catnip carrot. He played so hard that he finally fell asleep with the carrot next to him. The next thing we saw was a catnip carrot go sliding across the hardwood floor in the living room. It only stopped several feet later when it hit the edge of our fireplace hearth. The whole incident startled Benny because he was asleep and hadn't touched the carrot. By the way, our floors were perfectly level, so this could not be explained away by gravity. And once, while at our vacation condominium, we watched the movie *Madagascar 2*. The DVD came with a multicolored clown wig, which, as a joke, we placed on one of the large teddy bears sitting on the floor in the living room. While we were watching the movie, with Jackson asleep on the couch next to us and Benny sound asleep in the bedroom, the wig flew off the teddy bear. Jeff and I looked at each other and simultaneously said, "Clio?"

Another Clio sighting occurred at our condominium when Benny and Jackson were with me while the bathroom in our Indianapolis home was being renovated. I got up to go to the bathroom and noticed a dark-gray-(and possibly black)-and-white cat on the chair in the bedroom. "Hi, Benny," I said, only to walk out of the bedroom and see Benny coming from the kitchen. Benny does run fast, but there is no way he could have made it out to the kitchen and past me. When I looked back, there was no cat in the chair.

Clio's presence in our home continues to this day (even though we moved to a new house). A few years ago, we adopted a third cat, Trixie, from a friend when she moved into a nursing home. Almost daily, Trixie stands next to the box with Clio's ashes and stares at it. After a month, she started running through the house like someone was chasing her and now does that nearly every day. Although Trixie has a very distinct personality, over the past several years she has developed habits similar to Clio's, like antagonizing wildlife (fortunately from the great indoors), scratching in the same manner the basket that Clio scratched and looking back to see if we are watching, and loving attention when she does her one trick. Unlike Clio's one trick of doing somersaults, Trixie's idiosyncrasy is standing up on her hind legs and begging with her front paws. And like Clio, the more attention she receives when doing this, the more she does it. Although she hates wearing hats, she loves wearing a "Cleopatra hat," as if she knows she is definitely the new queen of the universe.

When Trixie first came into our lives, she would curl up like a normal cat for a nap. Now when she curls up, she often wraps both paws around her left hind leg and then goes to sleep. It's as if Clio has told Trixie to guard her hind leg because we might remove it. When Trixie's not clutching her leg, she covers her left eye before going to sleep, as if to protect it from us. Clio had lost both her left eye and left hind leg to cancer. Trixie, like Jackson, may very well have found a mentor in Clio.

According to Randy Russell, author of *Ghost Cats of the South*: "Cats are tied to place. No domestic animal is more territorial than the cat. When a cat moves in with a family, it likes to believe that it has found its 'forever home.' Forever means just that to a cat." For all Clio and Dickens did for me, I am delighted that I can provide them, and their spirits, a forever home.

Even though my heart was heavy with grief when Clio and Dickens passed, I came to realize that although their bodies were gone, their spirits were still with me. Of course, there is no definite proof that Clio and Dickens have returned to this earth as spirits, but these experiences, along with the many times cats have inexplicably shown up to save me, have made me believe that God or a higher being exists and there is an afterlife.

Clio and Dickens, like all my pets, have taught me valuable lessons and saved me repeatedly. So, is there an afterlife? We may never know while on this earth, but I am now convinced that there is one, and that our pets have souls. In fact, they may be little angels who come to earth to save us over and over again. Each animal is different and has his or her own personality. We provide our pets with a home and food, but they provide us with so much more. Their lives on earth are so short, but in that small span of time, they do more good for humankind than many people do in a much longer lifetime. I can't imagine that God intended a life or afterlife without them.

Clio, a runt of the litter who survived cancer twice, took me on an extraordinary journey that not only helped restore my self-esteem and confidence and allowed me to live, laugh, and love again, but provided me the greatest gifts of all—faith and hope. Her unique looks, her ability to overcome obstacles, and her unlimited self-esteem had a dramatic impact on my life. She was my one-eyed, three-legged therapist who helped me to reexamine my life. Yes, I grew up poor and without a father. Indeed, I didn't have nice clothes, my hair was unruly, and I was a few pounds overweight. And yes, I had virtually no self-esteem after being bullied in school and enduring an abusive marriage. Yet because of Clio, I, too, was able to overcome obstacles—and to realize that animals can provide us valuable lessons, save us during our low points, and change our lives forever.

I end this book and Clio's story with the poem "Heavenly Nap" by Ron Tranmer.

> *Your nine lives here have ended*
> *my loving furry friend,*
> *and you've been*
> *called to heaven*
> *to live life number ten.*
>
> *It's so hard to lose a pet*
> *who's loved as much as you,*
> *but God and all His angels*
> *are going to love you too.*
>
> *I'll bet you're lying peacefully*
> *upon an angel's lap.*
> *Purring there without a care,*
> *enjoying a heavenly nap.*
>
> *Oh how I will miss you.*
> *But time will pass and then,*
> *one day I'll call your name*
> *and you'll be on my lap again.*

Thank you, my dear friend and therapist, for all the love you gave me and all you have done for me. One day, I'll wake you from your "heavenly nap" and together we'll enjoy a can of tuna. By the way, Clio, don't worry—you can have most of it. Or maybe even all of it.

# Acknowledgments

FIRST AND FOREMOST, I WOULD LIKE TO THANK MY HUSBAND, JEFF, for his support and encouragement during the endless hours I spent writing this book and not with him. To my friends who believed this story was worth telling and encouraged me while I pursued its publication, I am deeply indebted.

I would like to extend a special thank you to author coach, marketing consultant, and fellow cat lover Mark Malatesta, who encouraged me to continue to pursue publication of this work and helped me to "think outside the box" about potential markets for the book.

Thank you to the staff of Purdue University Press, who have been a joy to work with. I extend special thanks to Justin Race, Andrea Gapsch, Chris Brannan, Katherine Purple, Kelley Kimm, Bryan Shaffer, and Janelle Boys-Chen.

I owe a true debt of gratitude to Clio's veterinarian, Dr. David Fenoglio, and his office staff at Augusta Animal Clinic, who saved her life over and over again and also understood how much this sweet cat meant to me. I am also grateful to the other veterinarians who treated and helped Clio. In fact, I greatly appreciate all veterinarians, who every day treat patients who can't tell them what is wrong, are incredibly frightened, and often don't appreciate why a strange person is poking and prodding them. This book is a tribute to their work. They do far more than save the lives of pets—they save the lives of pet parents.

Moreover, I am grateful to my late mother and father, who raised me to love animals and appreciate all their wonderful qualities and the friendship and inspiration they provide. Finally, I am grateful to all the animals in my life—both dogs and cats, including my current furry friends, Benny, Jackson, and Trixie—who have taught me so much and continue to inspire me. Most importantly, I am greatly indebted to Clio, my one-eyed, three-legged therapist, and her adoptive brother, Dickens, who helped me regain my self-esteem, renewed my belief in a higher being, and taught me to trust and love again.

# About the Author

KATHY M. FINLEY IS A LIFELONG ANIMAL LOVER WHO HAS A SPE-cial affinity for cats and cat rescue. Finley often thought she would become a veterinarian but couldn't face the possibility of being unable to save an animal's life, so she pursued a career that allowed her to use her talents for storytelling and writing. She is now using the skills she gleaned from her successful career in the nonprofit sector to advocate for animals by sharing how they have helped her put her own life in perspective and face life's everyday challenges.

During her professional life, Finley ran several nonprofit organizations and published extensively in the field of association management. In 2018 she was awarded the Albert Nelson Marquis Lifetime Achievement Award. She holds a PhD in organizational development and two master's degrees.

Finley has a blog titled *Cat Scratches and Scribbles* on her website, KathyFinley.com, where she posts monthly on subjects such as the human-animal bond, the health benefits that pets provide, and stories of pets who "rescued" their pet parents. She has also published guest blogs for Cat Care Solutions, Lola the Rescued Cat, Rescued by His Kingdom (for domestic abuse survivors), Paws for Reaction, and Elderly Pet and is an award-winning member of the Cat Writers' Association.

Finley volunteers extensively in her community through her service club, Altrusa International of Indianapolis, and has been a Toastmaster since 1994, achieving the highest Toastmaster Award, Distinguished

Toastmaster, twice. Her hobbies include walking, gardening, scrap-booking, and antiquing (especially for vintage cat collectibles). She and her husband, Jeff, live with their three cats, Benny, Jackson, and Trixie, in Indianapolis.

9 781612 498737